Writing the Critical Essay

GAY MARRIAGE

An **OPPOSING VIEWPOINTS®** Guide

Lauri S. Friedman, *Book Editor*

Christine Nasso, *Publisher*
Elizabeth Des Chenes, *Managing Editor*

OPPOSING
VIEWPOINTS®
SERIES

GREENHAVEN PRESS
An imprint of Thomson Gale, a part of The Thomson Corporation

THOMSON

GALE

Detroit • New York • San Francisco • New Haven, Conn. • Waterville, Maine • London

For more information, contact
Greenhaven Press
27500 Drake Rd.
Farmington Hills, MI 48331-3535
Or you can visit our Internet site at http://www.gale.com

LIBRARY OF CONGRESS CATALOGING-IN-PUBLICATION DATA

Gay marriage / Lauri S. Friedman, book editor.
   p. cm. — (Writing the critical essay)
  Includes bibliographical references and index.
  ISBN-13: 978-0-7377-3462-1 (hardcover)
  1. Same-sex marriage—United States. 2. Same-sex marriage. I. Friedman, Lauri S.
  HQ1034.U5G39 2008
  306.84'80973—dc22

                                        2007032360

ISBN-10: 0-7377-3462-0 (hardcover)
Printed in the United States of America

CONTENTS

Examining the state of writing and how it is taught in the United States was the official purpose of the National Commission on Writing in America's Schools and Colleges. The commission, made up of teachers, school administrators, business leaders, and college and university presidents, released its first report in 2003. "Despite the best efforts of many educators," commissioners argued, "writing has not received the full attention it deserves." Among the findings of the commission was that most fourth-grade students spent less than three hours a week writing, that three-quarters of high school seniors never receive a writing assignment in their history or social studies classes, and that more than 50 percent of first-year students in college have problems writing error-free papers. The commission called for a "cultural sea change" that would increase the emphasis on writing for both elementary and secondary schools. These conclusions have made some educators realize that writing must be emphasized in the curriculum. As colleges are demanding an ever-higher level of writing proficiency from incoming students, schools must respond by making students more competent writers. In response to these concerns, the SAT, an influential standardized test used for college admissions, required an essay for the first time in 2005.

Books in the Writing the Critical Essay: An Opposing Viewpoints Guide series use the patented Opposing Viewpoints format to help students learn to organize ideas and arguments and to write essays using common critical writing techniques. Each book in the series focuses on a particular type of essay writing—including expository, persuasive, descriptive, and narrative—that students learn while being taught both the five-paragraph essay as well as longer pieces of writing that have an opinionated focus. These guides include everything necessary to help students research, outline, draft, edit, and ultimately write successful essays across the curriculum, including essays for the SAT.

Using Opposing Viewpoints

This series is inspired by and builds upon Greenhaven Press's acclaimed Opposing Viewpoints series. As in the parent series, each book in the Writing the Critical Essay series focuses on a timely and controversial social issue that provides lots of opportunities for creating thought-provoking essays. The first section of each volume begins with a brief introductory essay that provides context for the opposing viewpoints that follow. These articles are chosen for their accessibility and clearly stated views. The thesis of each article is made explicit in the article's title and is accentuated by its pairing with an opposing or alternative view. These essays are both models of persuasive writing techniques and valuable research material that students can mine to write their own informed essays. Guided reading and discussion questions help lead students to key ideas and writing techniques presented in the selections.

The second section of each book begins with a preface discussing the format of the essays and examining characteristics of the featured essay type. Model five-paragraph and longer essays then demonstrate that essay type. The essays are annotated so that key writing elements and techniques are pointed out to the student. Sequential, step-by-step exercises help students construct and refine thesis statements; organize material into outlines; analyze and try out writing techniques; write transitions, introductions, and conclusions; and incorporate quotations and other researched material. Ultimately, students construct their own compositions using the designated essay type.

The third section of each volume provides additional research material and writing prompts to help the student. Additional facts about the topic of the book serve as a convenient source of supporting material for essays. Other features help students go beyond the book for their research. Like other Greenhaven Press books, each book in the Writing the Critical Essay series includes bibliographic listings of relevant periodical articles, books, Web sites, and organizations to contact.

Writing the Critical Essay: An Opposing Viewpoints Guide will help students master essay techniques that can be used in any discipline.

The Battle to Legalize Gay Marriage

Whether gay couples should be allowed to marry has been a topic of heated debate for many years, but the issue was freshly catapulted into the spotlight in 2003, when gay couples actively sought the right to marry in the state of Massachusetts. Though many had long dismissed claims that gay relationships be recognized on the same level as heterosexual ones, for the first time in history, the Massachusetts Supreme Court found differently. Justices voted 4–3 on November 18, 2003, that in the case of *Goodridge v. Dept. of Public Health,* Massachusetts may not "deny the protections, benefits and obligations conferred by civil marriage to two individuals of the same sex who wish to marry."[1] In other words, to continue to deny gay couples the rights that come with marriage constituted discrimination and the creation of a second-class citizenry, both of which the state's constitution prohibit.

After the state of Massachusetts legalized gay marriage, couples flocked there from all over the nation to obtain the licenses that would finally legitimize their relationships. But when the couples returned to their home states, they found that their local governments did not recognize the marriages as legal. The states were allowed to refuse the licenses under the Defense of Marriage Act (DOMA), passed under President Bill Clinton in 1996. DOMA prevents the federal government from recognizing same-sex marriages and allows individual states the right to not recognize a marriage between persons of the same sex, even if that marriage is legal in another state or even country. Using DOMA, therefore, the marriages became null and void once couples crossed state lines.

[1] Hillary GOODRIDGE & others vs. DEPARTMENT OF PUBLIC HEALTH & another. SJC-08860 Supreme Judicial Court of Massachusetts. November 18, 2003. http://www.law.umkc.edu/faculty/projects/ftrials/conlaw/Goodridge.html

Gay and lesbian couples rejoiced in Massachusetts in 2004 when they were allowed to legally wed.

This didn't deter those gay couples seeking marriage rights, however. In an unprecedented show of support for the gay community, judges and city officials in places such as San Francisco, California; New Paltz, New York; and Sandoval County, New Mexico went on a blitz, handing out marriage licenses to same-sex couples. People lined around the courthouse corner to obtain the licenses—in San Francisco alone 2,000 licenses were handed out in just four days. The mass celebration in the gay community was palpable from coast to coast; as one newlywed lesbian said, "I'm elated, I'm grateful, I'm honored that California is taking the stance behind all Americans' civil rights."[2] Yet the frenzy was quickly nipped in the bud when the local legislatures revoked the licenses on the grounds that they were in violation of the states' constitutions. The weddings in San Francisco, for example, were halted by the California Supreme Court on March 11, 2004, and were officially revoked on August 14, 2004. More than 4,000 licenses granted to same-sex couples instantly became null and void.

Watching the frenzy over same-sex weddings in various states across the nation was deeply troubling to certain conservatives, including President George W. Bush. In response to these actions, Bush proposed amending the U.S. Constitution to ban gay marriage by stating that marriage should be legal only between a man and a woman. The legislation he proposed was called the Federal Marriage Amendment (FMA), and in addition to prohibiting gay marriages it also proposed prohibiting the extension of marriage-like rights (such as those extended in domestic partnerships and civil unions) to same-sex couples, and also prevented people from having multiple spouses. As the amendment was written, "Marriage in the United States of America shall consist only of the union of a man and a woman.... Neither this constitution or the constitution of any state, nor state or federal law, shall be construed to require that marital status

2 Quoted in Rona Marech, "Couples: 'One step in a long road to equality,'" San Francisco Chronicle, March 15, 2005. http://www.sfgate.com/cgi-bin/article.cgi?f=/c/a/2005/03/15/REAX.TMP

or the legal incidents thereof be conferred upon unmarried couples or groups."[3]

The idea of amending the constitution to prohibit gay marriage was extremely controversial. Bush cast the issue as a matter of protecting the common good, saying passage of the amendment reflected the government's obligation to protect society. "Marriage cannot be severed from its cultural, religious and natural roots without weakening the good influence of society. Government, by recognizing and protecting marriage, serves the interests of all. Today I call upon the Congress to promptly pass, and send to the states for ratification, an amendment to our Constitution defining and protecting marriage as a union of man and woman as husband and wife."[4] Yet others, such as writer Joe Capello, saw the proposal of such an amendment as an attempt to create a class of second-rate citizens, in the same vein as blacks or women in previous eras of American history. Argued Capello, "Amending the Constitution in an attempt to permanently enshrine bigotry and discrimination is ... immoral."[5]

After several attempts, the Federal Marriage Amendment ultimately did not receive enough votes by the Congress to pass it into law. Though the FMA failed, the tide against same-sex marriage continued to sweep across the country. In the 2004 and 2006 elections, voters in 26 states approved ballot initiatives that created laws restricting marriage to between a man and a woman. The states that have passed gay marriage bans include Alabama, Alaska, Arkansas, Colorado, Georgia, Hawaii, Idaho, Kansas, Kentucky,

Many people, such as this protestor, believe marriage should only be allowed between male-female couples.

[3] S.J. Res. 40, the Federal Marriage Amendment, http://democrats.senate.gov/dpc/dpc-new.cfm?doc_name=lb-108-2-183.
[4] George W. Bush, "President Calls for a Constitutional Amendment Protecting Marriage," www.whitehouse.gov, February 24, 2004.
[5] Joe Capello, "Stop Hysteria over Gay Marriages," *Denver Post*, March 7, 2004.

Louisiana, Michigan, Mississippi, Missouri, Montana, Nebraska, Nevada, North Dakota, Ohio, Oklahoma, Oregon, South Carolina, South Dakota, Tennessee, Texas, Utah, Virginia, and Wisconsin. Many interpreted these sweeping passages as an outright condemnation of Congress's failure to federally protect heterosexual marriage; thus the states took it upon themselves to decree marriage as between a man and a woman only.

Yet a handful of states took the opportunity to articulate their support for same sex couples, if not through marriage, then by granting them many rights via either domestic partnerships or civil unions. These include property rights, health care rights, inheritance rights and tax rights, and many other significant benefits. Connecticut, New Jersey and Vermont grant civil unions to same-sex couples, while California, the District of Columbia, Hawaii, Maine, and Washington grant legal domestic partnerships. Furthermore, Illinois, Maine, New Hampshire, New York, and Rhode Island, among other states, have proposed civil union laws. While not marriages, "civil unions are the most politically stable answer for the next decade or so,"[6] according to law professor and same-sex marriage supporter Andrew Koppelman.

Massachusetts remains the nation's only state to have legal gay marriage. Whether other states and the federal government will agree on what marriage is and who should be covered under its rights-rich umbrella has yet to be determined as of 2007. But it was clear that the issue would remain contentious for some time to come. *Writing the Critical Essay: an Opposing Viewpoints Guide: Gay Marriage* exposes readers to the basic arguments made about gay marriage and helps them develop tools to craft their own essays on the subject.

[6] Andrew Koppelman, "Civil Conflict and Same-Sex Civil Unions," *Responsive Community*, Spring/Summer 2004.

Section One:
Opposing Viewpoints
on Gay Marriage

Gay Marriage Should Be Legal

Steven Lubet

In the following viewpoint, author Steven Lubet argues that gay marriage should be legal because it helps more people than it hurts. He tells the story of Nick and Stanley, a gay couple whose life was negatively impacted because of their inability to be lawfully wed. Despite suffering emotionally and financially, the couple stayed together for the duration of their lives, a testament to the power of love. Lubet holds up Nick and Stanley as an example of people whom gay marriage could have helped; he challenges readers to find an example in which a marriage between Nick and Stanley could have hurt anyone. Lubet concludes that most arguments against gay marriage are discriminatory and weak, and will not survive. Gay marriage, according to Lubet, will be legal at some point in the United States.

Steven Lubet is a professor of law at Northwestern University. He is the author of *Murder in Tombstone: The Forgotten Trial of Wyatt Earp*. His articles have appeared in periodicals such as *American Lawyer,* from which this viewpoint was taken.

Consider the Following Questions:

1. According to the author, how many states have statutes or constitutional provisions that restrict marriage to a man and a woman?
2. In what way are humans motivated by stories, according to Lubet?
3. Who is Alan Keyes and what is his opinion of gay marriage, according to the author?

Steven Lubet, "Chicago Story," *American Lawyer,* vol. 27, November 2005, pp. 178–79. Copyright © 2005 American Lawyer Media L. P. Reproduced by permission of the author.

It would be nice to think that "freedom means freedom for everybody," as Vice President Dick Cheney so memorably opined in his 2004 debate with Democratic candidate John Edwards. For same-sex couples in the United States, however, the freedom to marry exists only in Massachusetts. In much of the rest of the country, gay marriage seems more distant than ever. Forty-three states have statutes or constitutional provisions that limit marriage to "a man and a woman," and California governor Arnold Schwarzenegger recently vetoed a bill that would have allowed same-sex partners to wed.

Gay couples began holding formal ceremonies in Boston the very day a new law made it possible for them to legally marry.

Then again, it is always darkest before the dawn. There is actually a very good reason to believe that gay marriage will eventually be legalized in the United States, and not just because that would be the fair, progressive, and humane thing to do. You don't have to agree with Dick Cheney (and me) about the meaning of freedom in order to understand why gay marriage rights are almost certain to expand. You just have to know something about the power of stories.

The Power of Stories

We like to tell ourselves that people are persuaded by logical arguments based on facts, reasons, and morality. It is much more often the case, however, that people are persuaded by stories. As the linguist George Lakoff explains in his pithy book *Don't Think of an Elephant!*, it is all a matter of cognition. Human beings tend to be motivated by concrete images rather than abstractions. We typically reach decisions through a process of visualization and empathy—which Lakoff calls "metaphorical thought"—as opposed to purely rational (or even moral) deduction.

In other words, we use stories to make sense of the world, and the more vivid the better. Stories invite us (indeed, they impel us) to expand on our own experiences, to imagine the real-life consequences of individual and social choices, and—most importantly—to see ourselves in new or challenging situations. That is why photographs of starving children in Niger, or firsthand accounts of murder in Darfur, can spur world response in ways that logical appeals cannot. Everyone knows that famine and genocide are bad, but we start to take action when we can visualize the problem and therefore empathize with the victims. . . .

There is nothing inherently ideological about storytelling. It is accepted and exploited by advertisers, marketers, lawyers, and politicians of all stripes—though some use it more effectively than others. Nonetheless, the theory of "story power" can be used far more readily in support of gay rights than in opposition. Why? Because it is easy to tell stories about the human cost of antigay discrimination. And while it is obviously possible to make moral claims about the depravity of the "gay lifestyle," it is pretty hard to conceive of a story in which marriage (monogamy!) makes things worse.

Here is an example of a powerful story.

> ## The New Frontier of the Struggle for Civil Rights
>
> The fight for queer civil rights is as important to the 21st century as the fight for black civil rights was the 20th.
>
> Victoria A. Brownworth, "Civil Disobedience—Civil Rights," Curve, Vol. 14, June 2004.

One Powerful Story

My parents were always broad-minded and liberal, even in the early 1950s, when I was a small child. Their social circle included people of all racial and religious backgrounds, including intermarried couples, which was very unusual at the time. They were also friends with a same-sex couple, whom I will call Stanley and Nick (my dad worked with Stanley). Of course, in those days it was dangerous to be openly gay in Chicago—you could be fired, evicted, or beaten up—so Stanley and Nick were officially "roommates." Their closest friends figured out the true nature of their relationship, although no one ever spoke about it, especially at the office.

Stanley and Nick eventually moved to the East Coast, but they stayed in touch with my parents, exchanging birthday cards and occasional telephone calls.

"Can you believe it?" Stanley would say. "I still have the same roommate after all these years." "Incredible," my dad

A gay couple is showered with rice after obtaining a legal marriage license in Massachusettes in 2004.

would reply, knowing the secret but keeping up appearances. "Give Nick our best."

Marriage Improves Lives

In the early 1990s, Nick had a serious stroke requiring extended hospitalization and expensive follow-up care. Stanley's job provided medical insurance, but it did not cover Nick. Although they had lived as spouses for more than 40 years, they were legally unmarried and unrelated. As far as the insurance company was concerned, Nick and Stanley might as well have been complete strangers. They had to sell their house to pay the medical bills.

My father died a few years ago, and Stanley provided my mother with as much comfort as he could. Old friends are the best friends in times of sorrow, so they spoke often about their younger days when Stanley and my father worked together. One bittersweet phone call came on the occasion of Stanley's eightieth birthday.

"How are you celebrating?" my mother asked.

"I am going to drink a glass of wine," he said, "and then I am going to visit my partner in the nursing home."

That was the first time in over 50 years that she had ever heard Stanley acknowledge his lover as anything other than a roommate.

This is a persuasive story because it is specific and direct, evoking empathy for the difficulty of two men's lives. They stayed together in sickness and in health—not to mention discrimination and debt—but were never granted the comforts or advantages of legal recognition. Marriage would have made their lives better, while harming no one.

End of story.

Arguments Against Gay Marriage Will Fail

Now try to come up with a counterstory—not an argument or a set of dire predictions, but a plausible narrative, supported by vivid characterizations and believable details, in

American Attitudes on Gay Marriage

Although older Americans overwhelmingly oppose gay marriage, younger Americans tend to favor the idea.

An ABC News/Washington Post poll asked the following question:
Do you think it should be legal or illegal for homosexual couples to get married?

Date	Young Adults (18–30)			All Adults		
	Legal	Illegal	Other	Legal	Illegal	Other
August 2004	49%	48%	4%	32%	62%	5%
March 2004	63%	36%	1%	38%	59%	3%
February 2004	54%*	NR	NR	39%	55%	6%
January 2004	56%	42%	3%	41%	55%	4%
September 2003	51%*	46%*	3%*	37%	55%	8%

* Indicates results for ages 18–34

Taken from: ABC News/Washington Post

which people's lives are made worse by gay marriage. I'll bet that nothing immediately springs to mind.

Yes, I recognize that there are moral and religious objections to homosexuality. I understand that gay marriage is distasteful, even frightening, to many Americans who are not necessarily homophobic. My point is not so much that they are wrong, but rather that their arguments will ultimately fail.

During the 2004 Illinois Senate election, Republican candidate Alan Keyes justified his opposition to gay marriage by calling homosexuals selfish hedonists. The basis of marriage, he explained, must be more than selfishness, and thus the wedding of same-sex couples would debase the institution. For the moment, let's put aside Keyes's wobbly logic. His argument still lacks persuasive force because it is merely declarative. Gay marriage is bad and will lead to bad things, he insisted, but he could not provide a narrative, or even an anecdote, to support his claim. Even if he were right in the broad sense, there would still be no way to visualize the supposed ill effects of gay marriage.

Gay Marriage Will Be Legal Someday

And in any event, the tale of Stanley and Nick thoroughly undermines the image of gay couples as selfish hedonists. There is nothing that seems selfish or hedonistic about their generous and dedicated commitment to each other, which survived terribly hard times.

It can take a long time to change public opinion in a democracy, but the process is already under way in the case of gay rights. Antidiscrimination laws can be found everywhere; civil unions and domestic partnerships are now recognized in ways that would have been unthinkable even a decade ago. In large part, I think, storytelling is responsible for this transformation in attitudes, and the trend will surely continue, inconsistently but steadily, until Dick Cheney and I can agree that there really is "freedom for everybody."

Analyze the Essay:

1. The author used the story of Nick and Stanley as a vehicle to argue in favor of gay marriage. What elements of the story were most compelling to you? Do you think this was a powerful way for the author to make his point? Why or why not?

2. Steven Lubet argues that gay marriage does not hurt anyone; it only helps gay couples strengthen their commitment to each other. How do you think James E. Phelan, the author of the following viewpoint, would respond to this claim?

Gay Marriage Should Not Be Legal

James E. Phelan

In the following viewpoint, author James E. Phelan argues against making gay marriage legal. Phelan argues that gay relationships are not right for marriage, claiming that gay men leave relationships quickly and typically are unfaithful to their partners. Furthermore, he claims that lesbian relationships are prone to domestic violence, and that homosexuals in general are at high risk for disease, mental illness, and depression. If gay marriages were to be legalized, Phelan argues, the government and employers would have to pay millions of dollars in healthcare costs, spousal benefits, domestic violence, and divorce proceedings stemming from gay marriage cases. For all of these reasons, Phelan concludes that gay marriage should not be legal.

James E. Phelan is a Clinical Social Worker, and prolific researcher and writer on issues of human sexuality. He is a member of the Scholars for Social Justice, Catholic Central Union (Verein) of America.

Consider the Following Questions:

1. According to Phelan, what is the average length of homosexual relationships?
2. What does the word "embeddedness" mean in the context of the viewpoint?
3. What does Phelan warn gay marriage could lead to?

The "gay" marriage issue is currently the number one social topic today. The main plea from proponents to lawmakers is for them to legalize marriage between same genders. "Gays" and lesbians say they want to have the same legal matrimonial privileges that heterosexuals have. In leaps and bounds, they are getting through to lawmakers; a case in point is in the United States, where recently same-sex marriage was made "legal" in the Commonwealth of Massachusetts. There, the heterosexual marriage arena is already cumbered; an over-50% divorce rate has had a grave impact on society as a whole. To add to an already overburdened institution will inevitably make matters worse, especially given the homosexual's history, relational issues, and proclivities towards violence. . . .

Public Health Considerations

While the debate is about "rights," not "lifestyle," we must not silence the facts and ignore any consequential issues. According to the research, despite the knowledge of AIDS risk, homosexuals continue, time after time, to indulge in unsafe sex practices. Moreover, homosexuals represent the highest incidence of sexually transmitted disease cases (STDs) in the world.

The Talking Sex Project, conducted in Canada, found there was no impact of education on the knowledge of HIV risk through anal sex. "Gay" men will engage in unprotected anal intercourse time and time again, despite the consequences. In a nation-wide study in Canada, of 4,803 men recruited from gay-identified sources, 23% reported at least one episode of unprotected anal intercourse. In an earlier study entitled Men's Survey 91 tabulating the findings of 500 men from 35 cities in Canada, 62% of the respondents admitted participating in anal intercourse in the three months prior to the survey completion. The proportion of those who "never" used a condom was 12.2% for insertive anal intercourse, and 11.5% for receptive anal intercourse; given the risk of AIDS in the population (e.g., gays who go to public baths) those figures represent a significant risk factor in Canada. For example, high proportions of unprotected anal intercourse were found in many Canadian cities: Toronto (73.3%), Vancouver (56.3%), and Montreal (57.1%). . . .

Homosexuality and Mental Illness

There are many other things to consider as well. For example, over one third of homosexuals are substance abusers. Furthermore, they are more likely to suffer from gender identify confusion. They are also more likely to have mental health conditions such as eating disorders, personality disorders, paranoia, depression, and anxiety. In results from 186 self-identified women in Toronto who completed surveys that were compared to Canada's General Health Surveys, the comparisons found that lesbians drank more than heterosexuals and also had a higher incidence of mental health problems.

Gay Relationships Are Not Right for Marriage

Let's look at "gay" relationships in more detail, beyond what you will read in the popular media. Compared to heterosexual men, "gay" men report a shorter level of duration in their

Kris Mineau, director of the Massachusetts Family Institute, is among those who belive gay marriage should not be legalized.

longest relationship. Fewer heterosexual men have "open" (when either one or both partners are sexually non-exclusive) relationships compared to their "gay" counterparts. Ultimately, "gays" have fewer monogamous relationships. Their partners' sexual exclusivity is not an important factor in their relationships.

The famous study, The Male Couple, conducted by two homosexuals, one a psychologist and the other a psychiatrist, found that of the 156 couples studied, only seven had maintained sexual fidelity. Those couples that had maintained a relationship for more then five years were unable to maintain sexual fidelity. Although the study found that close to a third of the sample lived together longer than ten years, they also found that "the majority of couples ... and all the couples together longer than five years, were not continuously sexually exclusive with each other."

Other research found that the average length of homosexual relationships was only about two years. Others state that while many gay couples may stay together for a time, they become roommates bound chiefly by companionship and domestic ties, ceasing to be bed partners, and find sex (usually anonymous) outside the relationship. . . .

Gay Marriage Does Not Serve the Common Good

Gay marriage, like all the liberal ideas of the 1970s—including no-fault divorce, abortion on demand, cohabitation, and daycare—does not and cannot serve the common good.

Robert W. Patterson, "Why Gay Marriage Doesn't Measure Up," Human Events, March 22, 2004.

"Diametrically Opposite" of Marriage

Lesbians experience more "fusion" or "embeddedness" within their primary relationships, which occurs more frequently, and with greater intensity the longer the relationship is. The researchers found that each lesbian partner has no solid sense of self. At the same time, there is a problem of competition in the lesbian relationship. The problem occurs when one partner begins to feel that she has become lost in her partner, again a demonstration of "embeddedness."

America Opposes Gay Marriage

A Pew/PSRA poll found that the majority of Americans oppose legalizing gay marriage.

Do you strongly favor, favor, oppose, or strongly oppose . . . allowing gays and lesbians to marry legally?

Date	Young Adults (18–29)			All Adults			Sample/ Margin of Error	Dates
	Favor	Oppose	Other	Favor	Oppose	Other		
August 2004	40%	50%	10%	29%	60%	11%	1512 (±3%)	8/5–10
July 2004	NR	NR	NR	32%	56%	12%	2009 (±2.5%)	7/8–18
March 2004	47%	46%	7%	32%	59%	9%	1703 (±3%)	3/17–21
February 2004	41%	52%	7%	30%	63%	7%	1500 (±3%)	2/11–16
December 2003	45%	46%	9%	30%	63%	7%		
November 2003	53%	42%	5%	30%	62%	9%		
October 2003	45%	46%	9%	32%	59%	9%	1515 (±3%)	10/15–19
July 2003	52%	40%	8%	38%	53%	9%	1001 (±3%)	6/24–7/8
March 2001	52%	41%	7%	35%	57%	8%	2041 (±2.5%)	3/5–18
June 1996	42%	51%	7%	28%	65%	7%	1975 (±3%)	5/31–6/9

Taken from: Pew/PSRA

From these findings and others, it is clear to see that homosexuals are the diametrically opposite of heterosexuals overall. "Gay" men cannot commit to monogamy, and this will be an inevitable problem in the marriage arena. After the "honeymoon period," they will divert to an "open relationship" or tire of that, and seek divorce or just multiply lovers. Lesbians, on the other hand, lack solidity or stability in their relationships.

A plaintiff in the New Jersey case, Lewis v. Harris, *listens to the end of oral arguments in which seven same-sex couples sued the state for the right to marry.*

Lesbians Prone to Domestic Violence

For lesbians, domestic violence will be the highlight within the marriage. An already overburdened police force dealing with domestic violence will get more than they can handle.

Aggressive behaviour is legendary in homosexuality. Earlier research has shown a correlation between violence and homosexuality. It has estimated that same-sex relational battering occurs in as many as one in three relationships. Lesbians are especially violent in their relationships. In a sample of 279 female college students, lesbians were

generally more criminal and violent compared to heterosexual females.

In a study of lesbian victims, it was found that physical
violence, emotional abuse, and acts of intimidation do occur
with sufficient frequency within lesbian relationships. One
psychotherapist personally found lesbians to be terrorized
in their relationships. Patterns of violent incidents were com-
monplace in the lesbian relationship.

Gay Marriage's Slippery Slope

Given their history, "gay" men will not stay in monogamous relationships and therefore are not good candidates
for marriage. Lesbians, on the other hand, who may tend
to hold onto relationships, will not stop the cycle of violence, which, according to the research, is embedded within
them. Therefore, they too are not candidates for marriage.
Lawmakers and proponents need to consider these factors
when proposing to legalize these marriages. The aftermath
will be immense. The courts will be overwhelmed with cases
of domestic violence and infidelity. Employers will have to
fork out millions of dollars in healthcare costs and other
spousal benefits. . . .

Besides the relationship issues of infidelity and instability,
some proponents are even advocating for "three-way marriages." Dr. Jack Drescher, a medical doctor who is a gay
activist in the American Psychiatric Association, provided a
rationale for these relationships: "Our culture tells us that
we're supposed to find satisfaction in one person. But, not
everyone can find everything they need in one [person]."

Gay Marriages Slippery Slope

Finally, I would like the reader to think about what serious
aftermath same-sex marriage could bring on. While doing
so, it is important to consider the comments of one writer
who says that the comparison between same-sex marriage
and bisexual polygamous marriage is strikingly cogent.
The point is made that the person who claims legitimacy
for same-sex marriage, if he or she is to remain consistent,

could also claim legitimacy for bisexual polygamous marriage—thus exposing the fact that the basis of their position is not an affirmation of civil rights, but a nihilistic indifference toward fundamental values. Same-sex marriage proponents are aware of the attendant flood of culturally perverse legal challenges that recognizing same-sex marriage invites. Then on what credibly remaining basis will the Courts strike them down? Is this what society needs—a flood of perverse marriage variances?

Analyze the Essay:

1. In this essay, James E. Phelan opposes gay marriage on the basis it could lead to polygamous marriage, marriage between more than 2 people. In making this prediction, he uses what is called "slippery slope" reasoning—that allowing one act or event could send society careening down a slope to more acts or events. What is your opinion of slippery slope thinking? Do you that polygamy is a possible outcome of gay marriage? Why or why not?

2. Phelan claims that gay relationships only last a few years, and argues this should make gays ineligible for marriage. But Phelan also acknowledges that the divorce rate among heterosexuals is 50 percent, indicating that the relationships of many straight couples do not last a lifetime under marriage. What do you think—should how long a relationship lasts prequalify someone for marriage? Who should be eligible for marriage? Explain your answer using evidence from the text.

Gay Marriage Threatens Society

Charles Colson

In the following viewpoint, author Charles Colson argues that gay marriage threatens the very pillar upon which society rests: the stable family. Colson points to evidence that shows when children are raised without one gender of parent around, they are more likely to drop out of school, abuse substances, and commit crimes. Since gay marriage would necessarily result in couples of the same-sex, Colson reasons that children raised in such households would be troubled. Colson supports the Federal Marriage Amendment which stipulates that marriage is between a man and a woman, concluding that gay marriage could lead to increased crime and chaos and the eventual breakdown of society.

Charles Colson is the founder of Prison Fellowship Ministries, a religious-based outreach and criminal justice reform organization serving prisoners, ex-prisoners, and their children. His articles often appear in *Christianity Today,* from which this viewpoint was taken.

Consider the Following Questions:

1. What does the word "millennia" mean in the context of the viewpoint?
2. According to the author, what percentage of kids from broken families lead troubled lives?
3. What happened in Norway following the 1993 legalization of same-sex marriage in that country, according to Colson?

In 2004 fifty-three gay couples paid for marriage licenses in spite of being told by clerks that state law would not allow for their approval.

Is America witnessing the end of marriage? The Supreme Judicial Court of Massachusetts has ordered that the state issue marriage licenses to same-sex couples. (By late March [2004], the Massachusetts legislature voted to recognize same-sex civil unions instead.) An unprecedented period of municipal lawlessness has followed, with officials in California, New York, Oregon, and New Mexico gleefully mocking their state constitutions and laws. The result: Thousands of gays rushed to these municipalities to "marry," while much of the news media egged them on.

In the midst of the chaos, President Bush announced his support for a Federal Marriage Amendment, which assures

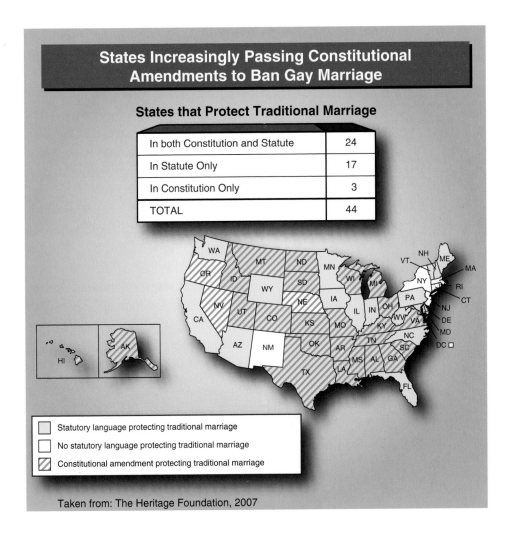

States Increasingly Passing Constitutional Amendments to Ban Gay Marriage

States that Protect Traditional Marriage

In both Constitution and Statute	24
In Statute Only	17
In Constitution Only	3
TOTAL	44

Statutory language protecting traditional marriage

No statutory language protecting traditional marriage

Constitutional amendment protecting traditional marriage

Taken from: The Heritage Foundation, 2007

that this contentious issue will be debated in every quarter of American life. It should be, because the consequences of having "gay marriage" forced on us by judicial (or mayoral) fiat will fall on all Americans—not just those who embrace it.

As a supporter of the amendment, I'm well aware of the critical arguments. As the president noted, "After more than two centuries of American jurisprudence, and millennia of human experience, a few judges and local authorities are presuming to change the most fundamental institution of civilization. Their action has created confusion on an issue that requires clarity."

He's right. Here's the clarity: Marriage is the traditional building block of human society, intended both to unite couples and bring children into the world.

Tragically, the sexual revolution led to the decoupling of marriage and procreation; same-sex "marriage" would pull them completely apart, leading to an explosive increase in family collapse, out-of-wedlock births—and crime. How do we know this?

In nearly 30 years of prison ministry, I've witnessed the disastrous consequences of family breakdown—in the lives of thousands of delinquents. Dozens of studies now confirm the evidence I've seen with my own eyes. Boys who grow up without fathers are at least twice as likely" as other boys to end up in prison. Sixty percent of rapists and 72 percent of adolescent murderers never knew or lived with their fathers.

> ## The Slippery Slope of Gay Marriage
>
> Once marriage is no longer confined to a man and a woman, it is impossible to exclude virtually any relationship between two or more partners of either sex—even non-human partners.
>
> Timothy J. Dailey, "The Slippery Slope of Same-Sex 'Marriage.'" Brochure published by the Family Research Council (available online at www.frc.org).

Even in the toughest inner-city neighborhoods, just 10 percent of kids from intact families get into trouble, but 90 percent of those from broken families do.

Girls raised without a father in the home are five times more likely to become mothers while still adolescents, children from broken homes have more academic and behavioral problems at school and are nearly twice as likely to drop out of high school.

Critics agree with this but claim gay "marriage" will not weaken heterosexual marriage. The evidence says they're wrong.

Stanley Kurtz of the Hoover Institution writes: "It follows that once marriage is redefined to accommodate same sex couples, that change cannot help but lock in and reinforce the very cultural separation between marriage and parenthood that makes gay marriage conceivable to begin with."

He cites Norway, where courts imposed same-sex "marriage" in 1993—a time when Norwegians enjoyed a low out-of-wedlock birth rate. After the imposition of same-sex "marriage," Norway's out-of-wedlock birth rate shot up as the link between marriage and childbearing was broken and cohabitation became the norm.

Gay "marriage" supporters argue that most family tragedies occur because of broken heterosexual marriages—including those of many Christians. They are right. We ought

Some people believe poor stability in homosexual relationships puts children at greater risk if gays are allowed to marry and adopt.

to accept our share of the blame, repent, and clean up our own house. But the fact that we have badly served the institution of marriage is not a reflection on the institution itself; it is a reflection on us.

As we debate the wisdom of legalizing gay "marriage," we must remember that, like it or not, there is a natural moral order for the family. History and tradition—and the teachings of Jews, Muslims, and Christians—support the overwhelming empirical evidence: The family, led by a married mother and father, is the best available structure for both child-rearing and cultural health.

This is why, although some people will always pair off in unorthodox ways, society as a whole must never legitimize any form of marriage other than that of one man and one woman, united with intention of permanency and the nurturing of children.

Marriage is not a private institution designed solely for the individual gratification of its participants. If we fail to enact a Federal Marriage Amendment, we can expect, not just more family breakdown, but also more criminals behind bars and more chaos in our streets.

Analyze the Essay:

1. Colson's argument hinges on the assumption that marriage is the cornerstone of civilization and society. Do you agree with this idea? Why or why not? Explain your answer in full.
2. In this viewpoint, Colson claims that gay marriage will cause an increase in crime and chaos. How do you think Sherman Stein, the author of the following viewpoint, would respond to this claim?

Gay Marriage Helps Society

Sherman Stein

Extending marriage to gay couples will help strengthen society, argues Sherman Stein in the following viewpoint. Stein contends that gay marriage can reinforce the important values of trust, commitment, and partnership, which are important to society as a whole. The author points out that gay marriage does not threaten the relationships straight people have with their spouses or children; it only serves to increase the number of people in committed relationships. Stein concludes that when more people are bound by committed and loving relationships, society is strengthened and the world becomes a better place.

Sherman Stein is a former mathematics professor at the University of California, Davis.

> ## Consider the Following Questions:
> 1. What does Stein consider to be "practically a miracle?"
> 2. What comparison does the author make between gay marriage and the struggle for equal voting rights in the 20th century?
> 3. What point is the author making when he says, "No one is invading my home or kidnapping my wife and children?"

A quarter of a century ago, our then-teenage daughter, the youngest of our three children, announced that she was gay. Her revelation came as a shock, but the intervening years have given me time to reflect on homosexuality. I have slowly gone from that initial shock to acceptance, along the way reaching some insights.

Sherman Stein, "Marriage Can Be Expanded," *Los Angeles Times*, www.latimes.com, June 5, 2004. Reproduced by permission of the author.

We Need Not Fear Gay Marriage

In our world, the word "stranger" calls forth fear. For two people to shift from strangers to friends to devoted lifetime companions is practically a miracle. Society should encourage such commitments, which not only sustain two people but provide a firm foundation for our society.

All my life I had lived with the idea that "marriage" referred to a man and a woman. Now I wondered, why couldn't the gay world settle for "civil union" with all the legal benefits of marriage. Give us straight people time to adjust to "civil union," then gradually replace that word with "marriage." We need time to absorb new ideas.

Gay Marriage Does Not Threaten Straight Marriage

A 2004 study that compared U.S. divorce rates with divorce rates in Scandinavia (where gay partnerships are legal) concluded there was no evidence to suggest that giving partnership rights to same-sex couples in Scandinavia had any impact on heterosexual couples there.

Taken from: M.V. Badget, "Will Providing Marriage Rights to Same-Sex Couples Undermine Heterosexual Marriage?" Council on Contemporary Families and the Institute for Gay and Lesbian Strategic Studies, July 2004

Gay Marriage Does Not Threaten Straight Marriage

I am in the 54th year of a happy marriage. I do not feel that my marriage is threatened by expanding the meaning of the word "marriage." No one is invading my home or kidnapping my wife or children. Nor is the institution of marriage threatened. That people of the same sex might unite in a bond of trust is a far less serious threat to the institution of marriage than the need for both partners to hold down full-time jobs.

Slowly or abruptly, the meanings of words change. Think of the word "vote." Initially, the vote was restricted to men with property. Then it was expanded to include men who had established residency. By the beginning of the Civil War, almost all adult white males could vote. Next, with the pas-

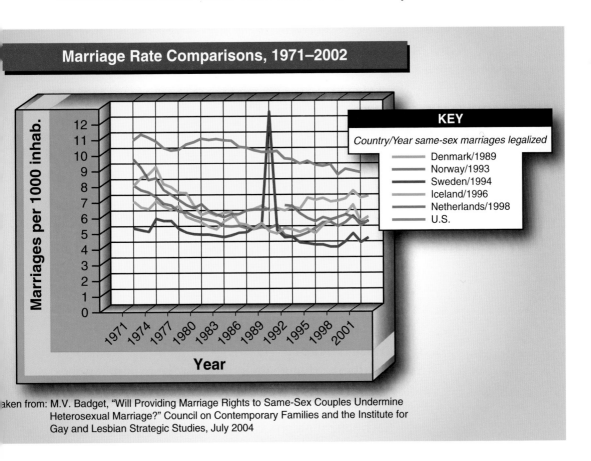

Marriage Rate Comparisons, 1971–2002

KEY

Country/Year same-sex marriages legalized

— Denmark/1989
— Norway/1993
— Sweden/1994
— Iceland/1996
— Netherlands/1998
— U.S.

Marriages per 1000 inhab.

Year

aken from: M.V. Badget, "Will Providing Marriage Rights to Same-Sex Couples Undermine Heterosexual Marriage?" Council on Contemporary Families and the Institute for Gay and Lesbian Strategic Studies, July 2004

Supporters of gay marriage rights believe that allowing couples to legally marry would help provide greater stability for them and their families.

sage of the 15th Amendment, blacks, in theory, had the right to vote. Women were granted the vote in 1920. Finally, the vote was extended to everyone 18 years old and over.

The More Committed People, the Stronger Society

There is an underlying similarity between expanding the embrace of the word "vote" and expanding the embrace of the word "marriage." But there is also an important difference. Each time the right to vote was extended, those who already had that right were indeed threatened. They could still vote, but their vote had less impact. But permitting two people of the same sex to form a union graced by the word "marriage" does not jeopardize those already married. It does not dilute the strength of an existing marriage, just as expanding the right to vote did not dilute the value of existing votes.

I do not understand why some of us are heterosexual and others are homosexual. Why are two of my children heterosexual and one homosexual? After decades of research, it is agreed that people do not choose their sexual orientation. I hope that some day we will look upon sexual orientation

Proponents of gay marriage argue that homosexuals can help society by adopting and raising children.

For the Good of Us All

I think it's a safe bet that marriage and the prospect of marriage would improve gay people's health and happiness and general welfare much as it has improved straight people's; I believe it will ennoble and dignify gay love and sex as it has done straight love and sex; I believe it will close the book on the culture of libertinism and liberation and replace it with a social compact forged of responsibility. ... If you insist on denying perhaps 12 million American homosexuals any hope of marrying, require yourself to consider how you would feel about denying marriage to 12 million heterosexuals [about the size of the state of Illinois]. Nothing less is worthy of them or of you.

Jonathan Rauch, *Gay Marriage: Why It Is Good for Gays, Good for Straights, and Good for America.* New York: Owl Books, p. 71.

with the same indifference we give to whether one is right- or left-handed. If we attain that state, we will all be living in a more compassionate world, one with less fear and animosity. Extending the meaning of the word "marriage" will not cause the straight to convert to gay, any more than it would the right-handed person to switch to left-handed.

If we were able to accept the ever-broadening meaning of the vote, which at each stage did threaten the existing order, we can surely absorb the extension of marriage, which will only strengthen the bonds that hold our society together.

Analyze the Essay:

1. Sherman Stein begins his essay by announcing that his daughter is gay. What bearing do you think this fact might have on his opinion of gay marriage? Do you think it makes his argument more or less credible, or has no bearing at all? Explain your answer in full.

2. Sherman Stein and Charles Colson disagree on whether gay marriage threatens society. However, both authors agree that marriage itself is a key ingredient to a healthy society. In your opinion, is the tradition of marriage instrumental to a strong society? Why or why not?

Gay Marriage Helps Children

Dale Carpenter

In the following viewpoint, author Dale Carpenter argues that being raised by gay parents does not hurt children, as is commonly claimed by opponents of gay marriage. Carpenter cites studies that show that being raised by gay parents does not harm, and can even help children develop positively. Carpenter realizes that no one is going to take children from gay parents: so the issue for him becomes whether it would be better for children to be raised by a married same-sex couple or an unmarried same-sex couple. Marriage helps all people to feel more secure and connected to each other, and therefore Carpenter believes marriage should be extended to same-sex couples for the benefit of their children.

Dale Carpenter is a professor at the University of Minnesota Law School, where he teaches courses on Sexual Orientation and the Law, the First Amendment, and Commercial Law. He also writes a regular column, "OutRight," for several gay publications across the country.

Consider the Following Questions:

1. What is the only state to prohibit gay couples from adopting children, according to the author?
2. How many children are currently being raised by gay parents, as reported by Carpenter?
3. What did sociologists Judith Stacey and Timothy Biblarz find about gay parenting, according to Carpenter?

Dale Carpenter, "Gay Marriage Helps Children," *Bay Area Reporter*, April 1, 2004. Reproduced by permission.

Many opponents of gay marriage do so on the grounds that marriage exists primarily for raising children, and that gay couples cannot satisfy this purpose. A strong version of this point holds that gay parents are incompetent to raise children, and perhaps are even dangerous to them (the "*competence* argument"). A milder version claims that opposite-sex married couples are optimal for child-rearing (the "*optimality* argument"). The competence argument is factually unsupported, and contravened by the laws of every state. The optimality argument may or may not be correct, but either way is irrelevant to the controversy over gay marriage.

Making same-sex marriage legal throughout the United States could benefit children growing up in a homosexual household where the parents are bound together legally.

What Opponents of Gay Marriage Assert

The competence argument asserts that children raised by gay parents, as compared to those raised by heterosexual parents, are:

- at higher risk emotionally and cognitively;
- are more apt to be confused about their sexual and gender identity; and
- are more likely to be molested.

Gays, therefore, ought not to raise children.

Since marriage includes a presumptive right to have and raise children, either through conception or adoption, gays ought to be denied marriage. The happiness and needs of gay couples do not justify putting children at risk.

Homosexuals Make Good Parents

If the competence argument is correct, states should bar gays altogether from parenting. Yet while judges sometimes use homosexuality as one factor among many in making custody and visitation determinations, *no state categorically bars gays from raising children*. Only one state, Florida, prohibits gays from adopting children. However, even Florida permits gays to raise their own biological children, to obtain custody of children, and to be long-term foster parents. In short, no state has made the policy judgment embodied by the competence argument.

In fact, the strong trend in the country is toward the relaxation of rules disfavoring gay parenting. About half of the states now recognize two-parent adoptions in which same-sex partners both adopt a child. Gay parenting is common. More than one million children are now being raised by gay parents, singly or in couples, in this country. According to the 2000 census, about one-fourth of all same-sex-couple households include children.

The available studies on the effects of gay parenting, while not methodologically perfect, seriously undermine the competence argument. While the studies may not yet prove that gays are just as good as heterosexuals at raising children, they point strongly to the conclusion that gays are at least minimally competent parents.

"No Measurable Effect"

In a review of 21 studies of gay parenting, sociologists Judith Stacey and Timothy Biblarz concluded that "every relevant study to date shows that parental sexual orientation per se has no measurable effect on the quality of parent-child relationships or on children's mental health or social adjustment." The minor observed differences between children raised by gay parents and those raised by straight parents "either favor children raised by lesbigay parents, are secondary effects of social prejudice, or represent 'difference' of the sort democratic societies should respect and protect." While more work must be done to shore up these conclusions, a strong provisional judgment can be made that the competence argument is factually baseless.

Gay Parents Do Not Negatively Affect Children

No differences have been found in personality measures, peer group relationships, self-esteem, behavioral difficulties, academic success and quality of family relationships [in children raised by homosexual parents]. The studies suggest only one meaningful difference: Children of lesbian parents are "more tolerant of diversity and more nurturing toward younger children than children whose parents are heterosexual."

Brad Sears and Alan Hirsch, "Straight-Out Truth on Gay Parents," *Los Angeles Times*, April 4, 2004.

No Good Data for Direct Comparisons

A milder version of the child-rearing objection to gay marriage maintains that even if gays should not be completely barred from parenting, married heterosexual couples should be strongly preferred. This optimality argument holds that, all else being equal, children do best when raised by a married mother and father.

In contrast to the competence argument, there is at least some empirical basis for the optimality argument. There is substantial evidence that children raised in married households are on average happier, healthier, and wealthier than children raised by single parents or by unmarried cohabiting

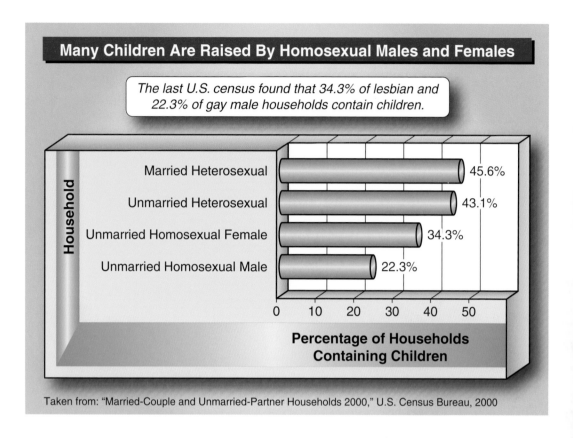

Many Children Are Raised By Homosexual Males and Females

The last U.S. census found that 34.3% of lesbian and 22.3% of gay male households contain children.

Household

Married Heterosexual	45.6%
Unmarried Heterosexual	43.1%
Unmarried Homosexual Female	34.3%
Unmarried Homosexual Male	22.3%

0   10   20   30   40   50

**Percentage of Households
Containing Children**

Taken from: "Married-Couple and Unmarried-Partner Households 2000," U.S. Census Bureau, 2000

parents. This probably has something to do with the legal and social support marriage provides.

Still, this is shaky empirical support for the optimality argument. There is no good study comparing children raised in married households with children raised by same-sex couples. And, because gay marriage is forbidden, there is no study comparing children raised by opposite-sex married couples with children raised by same-sex married couples.

Let's assume, for the sake of argument, that opposite-sex married couples provide the optimal environment for child-rearing. That is still no argument against gay marriage. First, even if a primary purpose of marriage is to facilitate child-rearing, it is not an indispensable purpose, as the many childless married couples can attest.

Being adopted by same-sex couples may help children develop positively and become more open-minded.

Many Children Need Loving, Married Parents

Second, gay marriage won't take any children from mothers and fathers who want to raise them. Consider: there is no shortage of children in the country. There are not enough married couples to raise them all. That's why states allow sub-optimal parenting by singles (gay and straight) and unmarried couples (gay and straight). Almost everyone agrees these sub-optimal arrangements are better than orphanages or foster care, where the outcomes for children are often terrible.

No serious person advocates removing all children from gay parents. So whether or not gay marriage is allowed, children will continue to be raised by gay parents. The only question is, Will these children be raised in homes that may enjoy the protections and benefits of marriage? If it's better for children to be raised by a married opposite-sex couple than by an unmarried opposite-sex couple, it would surely be better for children to be raised by a married same-sex couple than by an unmarried same-sex couple. That's the relevant comparison, not the comparison of married straight couples to gay couples.

If it's really concern for children that's motivating opponents of gay marriage, they ought to rethink their conclusion. They should be pounding the table for gay marriage.

Analyze the Essay:

1. To make his argument, Dale Carpenter spends extensive time explaining the position of his opponents. What did you think of this tactic? Does it confuse his essay or help clarify his points? Explain your opinion on whether this type of approach is useful or not.

2. What quotes did Dale Carpenter use to support his points about gay marriage? What qualifications do his speakers have?

Gay Marriage Hurts Children

Maggie Gallagher and Joshua K. Baker

In the following viewpoint, authors Maggie Gallagher and Joshua K. Baker argue that children should not be raised by gay parents. Gallagher and Baker cite studies that show when children are not raised by their mother and father they are more likely to fail in school, commit crime, experience sexual and physical abuse, not attend college, experience divorce as adults, have unwanted pregnancies, have substance abuse problems, and lead less physically healthy lives than children who are raised by both of their parents. Furthermore, they argue that studies which show gay parents have a positive affect on children are methodologically flawed. For these reasons they conclude that gay households are not ideal places for children to grow up.

Maggie Gallagher is President of the Institute for Marriage and Public Policy and a co-author of *The Case for Marriage*. Joshua Baker is the vice president of the Institute for Marriage and Public Policy.

Consider the Following Questions:

1. What did a *Child Trends* research brief find, and how do the authors use it to support their main argument?
2. Who is Evan Wolfson and what is his opinion of the affect of gay marriage on children?
3. What serious methodological flaw did the authors find in studies that found no evidence that gay marriage hurts children?

Maggie Gallagher and Joshua K. Baker, "Do Mothers and Fathers Matter?" *iMAPP Policy Brief*, February 27, 2004, pp. 1–3. Reproduced by permission.

In the last thirty years, thousands of studies evaluating the consequences of marriage have been conducted in various disciplines (e.g., psychology, sociology, economics, and medicine). Twelve leading family scholars recently summarized the research literature this way: "Marriage is an important social good associated with an impressively broad array of positive outcomes for children and adults alike. . . . [W]hether American society succeeds or fails in building a healthy marriage culture is clearly a matter of legitimate public concern." Among their conclusions:

- Marriage increases the likelihood that children enjoy warm, close relationships with parents.
- Cohabitation is not the functional equivalent of marriage.
- Children raised outside of intact married homes are more likely to divorce or become unwed parents themselves.
- Marriage reduces child poverty.
- Divorce increases the risk of school failure for children, and reduces the likelihood that they will graduate from college and achieve high status jobs.
- Children in intact married homes are healthier, on average, than children in other family forms.
- Babies born to married parents have sharply lower rates of infant mortality.
- Children from intact married homes have lower rates of substance abuse.
- Divorce increases rates of mental illness and distress in children, including the risk of suicide.
- Boys and young men from intact married homes are less likely to commit crimes.
- Married women are less likely to experience domestic violence than cohabiting and dating women.

- Children raised outside of intact marriages are more likely to be victims of both sexual and physical child abuse.

Mothers and Fathers Give Children Advantages In Life

They conclude, "Marriage is more than a private emotional relationship. It is also a social good. Not every person can or should marry. And not every child raised outside of marriage is damaged as a result. But communities where good-enough marriages are common have better outcomes for children, women, and men than do communities suffering from high rates of divorce, unmarried childbearing, and high-conflict or violent marriages."

A Multitude of Organizations Agree

Recent analyses by mainstream child welfare organizations confirm this consensus on the social evidence matters across ideological and partisan lines. For example:

- A *Child Trends* research brief summed up the scholarly consensus: "Research clearly demonstrates that family structure matters for children, and the family structure that helps the most is a family headed by two-biological parents in a low-conflict marriage. Children in single-parent families, children born to unmarried mothers, and children in stepfamilies or cohabiting relationships face higher risks of poor outcomes. . . . There is thus value for children in promoting strong, stable marriages between biological parents."
- An Urban Institute scholar concludes, "Even among the poor, material hardships were substantially lower among married couple families with children than among other families with children. . . . The marriage impacts were quite huge, generally higher than the

effects of education. The impacts [of marriage] were particularly high among non-Hispanic black families."

- A Centers for Disease Control report notes, "Marriage is associated with a variety of positive outcomes, and dissolution of marriage is associated with negative outcomes for men, women, and their children."
- A Center for Law and Social Policy Brief concludes, "Research indicates that, on average, children who grow up in families with both their biological parents in a low-conflict marriage are better off in a number of ways than children who grow up in single-, step-, or cohabiting-parent households."

The Biological Family Matters

While scholars continue to disagree about the size of the marital advantage and the mechanisms by which it is conferred, the weight of social science evidence strongly supports the idea that family structure matters and that the family structure that is most protective of child well-being is the intact, biological, married family.

The Social Science of Gay Parenting: A Competing Body of Evidence?

Most of the research on family structure, however, does not directly compare children in intact married homes with children raised from birth by same-sex couples. Thus the powerful new consensus on family structure is on a collision course with a separate emerging consensus from a related field: the social science literature on sexual orientation and parenting.

Judith Stacey summed up this new challenge to the social science consensus on family structure in testimony before the U.S. Senate this way:

The research shows that what places children at risk is not fatherlessness, but the absence of economic and social resources that a qualified second parent can provide, whether male or female. . . . Moreover, the research on children raised by lesbian and gay parents demonstrates that these children do as well if not better than children raised by heterosexual parents. Specifically, the research demonstrates that children of same-sex couples are as emotionally healthy and socially adjusted and at least as educationally and socially successful as children raised by heterosexual parents.

Other researchers, including at least two prominent professional associations, have made similar claims. Advocates for same-sex marriage often rely on these studies to assert that scientific evidence shows that married mothers and fathers hold no advantages for children. As Mary Bonauto, counsel for the plaintiffs in the Massachusetts marriage litigation, wrote in the Summer 2003 edition of *Human Rights*, "[C]hild-rearing experts in the American Academy of Pediatrics, the American Psychiatric Association, and the American Psychological Association insist that the love and commitment of two parents is most critical for children—not the parents' sex or sexual orientation."

Similarly Evan Wolfson, head of Freedom to Marry, asserted recently, "[T]here is no evidence to support the offensive proposition that only one size of family must fit all. Most studies—including the ones that [Maggie] Gallagher relies on—reflect the common sense that what counts is not the family structure, but the quality of dedication, commitment, self-sacrifice, and love in the household."

Weighing the Evidence

How should legal thinkers and decision-makers evaluate such competing claims about family structure and child well-being both allegedly grounded in social science evidence?

Numerous reviews of the literature on sexual orientation and parenting have been conducted. At least three such reviews have pointed to the serious scientific limitations of the social science literature on gay parenting.

Perhaps the most thorough review was prepared by Steven Nock, a sociologist at the University of Virginia who was asked to review several hundred studies as an expert witness for the Attorney General of Canada. Nock concluded:

> Through this analysis I draw my conclusions that 1) all of the articles I reviewed contained at least one fatal flaw of design or execution; and 2) not a single one of those studies was conducted according to general accepted standards of scientific research.

Letting Children Suffer for the Selfish Desires of Adults

Once we abandon marriage to the whims and desires of adults seeking validation of their sexual lifestyles, we denigrate children and their needs—legally validating relationships that would deliberately leave them motherless or fatherless. And that hurts society. We have plenty of data to show what happens to children when they grow up without a father or a mother. Prisons are filled with adults who were fatherless as children. The financial burden of welfare and prison programs on society as a result of children growing up without their mother or their father is horrific. And that is not even taking into consideration the immense personal suffering that inevitably is too often hidden behind these statistics.

Sharon Slater, "How Does Legalizing Same-Sex Marriage Hurt Marriage, Children and Society?" *Meridian Magazine*, 2004. http://www.meridian-magazine.com/ideas/041014Legalizing.html.

Design flaws researchers have found in these studies include very basic limitations:

a. **No nationally representative sample.** Even scholars enthusiastic about unisex parenting, such as Stacey and Biblarz, acknowledge that "there are no studies of child development based on random, representative samples of [same-sex couple] families."

Anti-gay marriage advocates believe children are at risk from not having both male and female role models in the home when raised by same-sex couples.

b. **Limited outcome measures.** Many of the outcomes measured by the research are unrelated to standard measures of child well-being used by family sociologists (perhaps because most of the researchers are developmental psychologists, not sociologists).

c. **Reliance on maternal reports.** Many studies rely on a mother's report of her parenting skills and abilities, rather than objective measures of child outcomes.

d. **No long-term studies.** All of the studies conducted to date focus on static or short-term measures of child development. Few or none follow children of unisex parents to adulthood.

We Need Mothers *and* Fathers

But perhaps the most serious methodological critique of these studies, at least with reference to the family structural debate, is this:

The vast majority of these studies compare single lesbian mothers to single heterosexual mothers. As sociologist Charlotte Patterson, a leading researcher on gay and lesbian parenting, recently summed up, "[M]ost studies have compared children in divorced lesbian mother-headed families with children in divorced heterosexual mother-headed families."

Most of the gay parenting literature thus compares children in some fatherless families to children in other fatherless family forms. The results may be relevant for some legal policy debates (such as custody disputes) but, in our opinion, they are not designed to shed light on family structure per se, and cannot credibly be used to contradict the current weight of social science: family structure matters, and the family structure that is most protective of a child's well-being is the intact, married biological family.

Children do best when raised by their own married mother and father.

Analyze the Essay:

1. To make their argument that children should be raised by mothers and fathers, Gallagher and Baker include quotes from experts who believe that children raised in gay households can fare as well as those in straight households. Does this inclusion undermine their argument? Why, if the authors are arguing against this point, do you think they chose to include such information? Explain your answer in full.

2. The authors of this viewpoint are members of the Institute for Marriage and Public Policy, a think tank that strongly opposes gay marriage. Does knowing their professional background influence the way you interpret their argument? If so, in what way?

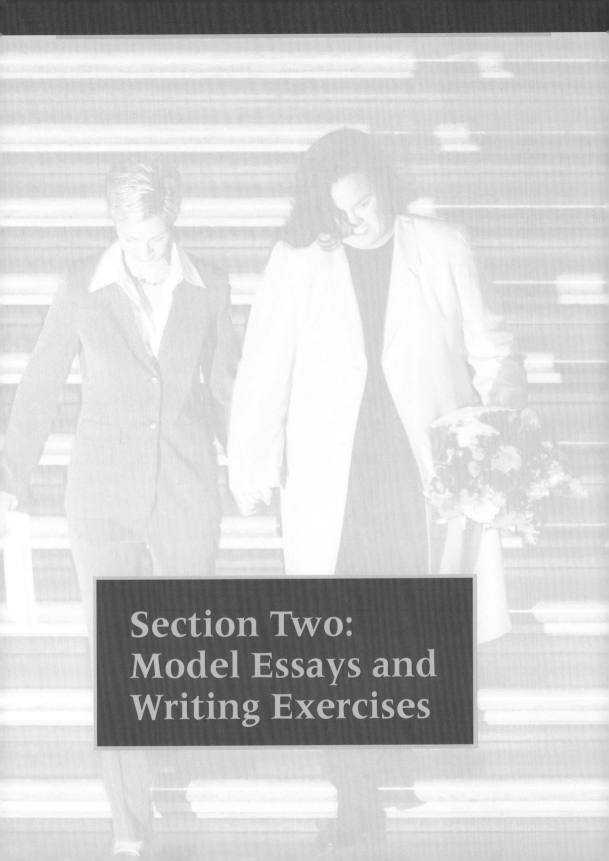

**Section Two:
Model Essays and
Writing Exercises**

The Five-Paragraph Essay

An *essay* is a short piece of writing that discusses or analyzes one topic. The five-paragraph essay is a form commonly used in school assignments and tests. Every five-paragraph essay begins with an *introduction,* ends with a *conclusion,* and features three *supporting paragraphs* in the middle.

The Thesis Statement. The introduction includes the essay's thesis statement. The thesis statement presents the argument or point the author is trying to make about the topic. The essays in this book all have different thesis statements because they are making different arguments about gay marriage.

The thesis statement should clearly tell the reader what the essay will be about. A focused thesis statement helps determine what will be in the essay; the subsequent paragraphs are spent developing and supporting its argument.

The Introduction. In addition to presenting the thesis statement, a well-written introductory paragraph captures the attention of the reader and explains why the topic being explored is important. It may provide the reader with background information on the subject matter or feature an anecdote that illustrates a point relevant to the topic. It could also present startling information that clarifies the point of the essay or put forth a contradictory position that the essay will refute. Further techniques for writing an introduction are found later in this section.

The Supporting Paragraphs. The introduction is then followed by three (or more) supporting paragraphs. These are the main body of the essay. Each subtopic is spearheaded by a topic sentence and supported by the essay's thesis statement. Each subtopic is then supported with its own facts, details, and examples. The writer can use various kinds of supporting material and details to back up the topic of each supporting paragraph. These may include statistics, quotations from people with special knowledge or expertise, historic facts, and anecdotes. A rule of writing is that specific and concrete examples are more convincing than vague, general, or unsupported assertions.

The Conclusion. The conclusion is the paragraph that closes the essay. Its function is to summarize or reiterate the main idea of the essay. It may recall an idea from the introduction or briefly examine the larger implications of the thesis. Because the conclusion is also the last chance a writer has to make an impression on the reader, it is important that it not simply repeat what has been presented elsewhere in the essay but close it in a clear, final, and memorable way.

Although the order of the essay's component paragraphs is important, they do not have to be written in the order presented here. Some writers like to decide on a thesis and write the introduction paragraph first. Other writers like to focus first on the body of the essay, and write the introduction and conclusion later.

Although the order of the essay's component paragraphs is important, they do not have to be written in the order presented here. Some writers like to decide on a thesis and write the introduction paragraph first. Other writers like to focus first on the body of the essay, and write the introduction and conclusion later.

Pitfalls to Avoid

When writing essays about controversial issues such as gay marriage, it is important to remember that disputes over the material are common precisely because there are many different perspectives. Remember to state your arguments in careful and measured terms. Evaluate your topic fairly—avoid overstating negative qualities of one perspective or understating positive qualities of another. Use examples, facts, and details to support any assertions you make.

The Persuasive Essay

There are many types of essays, but in general, they are usually short compositions in which the writer expresses and discusses an opinion about something. In the persuasive essay the writer tries to persuade (convince) the reader to do something or to agree with the writer's opinion about something. Examples of persuasive writing are easy to find. Advertising is one common example. Through commercial and print ads, companies try to convince the public to buy their products for specific reasons. Much everyday writing is persuasive, too. Letters to the editor, posts from sports fans on team Web sites, even handwritten notes urging a friend to listen to a new CD—all are examples of persuasive writing.

The Tools of Persuasion

The writer of the persuasive essay uses various tools to persuade the reader. Here are some of them:

- *Facts and statistics.* A fact is a statement that no one, typically, would disagree with. It can be verified by information in reputable resources, such as encyclopedias, almanacs, government Web sites, or reference books about the topic of the fact.

Examples of Facts and Statistics

- Americans celebrate their nation's birth every Fourth of July.
- Sacramento is the capital of California.
- The average American eats 252 eggs each year.
- A 2005 survey by the Science Museum in London found that 1 in 15 people have reported seeing a UFO.

It is important to note that facts and statistics can be *misstated* (written down or quoted incorrectly), *misinterpreted* (not understood correctly by the user), or *misused* (not used fairly). But, if a writer uses facts and statistics properly, they can add authority to the writer's essay.

- *Opinions.* An opinion is what a person thinks about something. It can be contested or argued with. However, opinions of people who are experts on the topic or who have personal experience are often very convincing. Many persuasive essays are written to convince the reader that the writer's opinion is worth believing and acting on.
- *Testimonials.* A testimonial is a statement given by a person who is thought to be an expert or who has another trait people admire, such as being a celebrity. Television commercials frequently use testimonials to convince watchers to buy the products they are advertising.
- *Examples and anecdotes.* An example is something that is representative of a group or type ("red" is an example of the group "color"). Examples are used to help define, describe, or illustrate something to make it more understandable. Anecdotes are extended examples. They are little stories with a beginning, middle, and end. They can be used just like examples to explain something or to show something about a topic.
- *Appeals to reason.* One way to convince readers that an opinion or action is right is to appeal to reason or logic. This often involves the idea that if some ideas are true, another must also be true. Here is an example of one type of appeal to reason:

The Humane Society rescues many animals every year. The Humane Society needs money to keep operating. Therefore, if you love animals, you should contribute money to the Humane Society.

- *Appeals to emotion.* Another way to persuade readers to believe or do something is to appeal to their emotions—love, fear, pity, loyalty, and anger are some of the emotions to which writers appeal. A writer who wants to persuade the reader that gay marriage should be legal might appeal to the reader's sense of love and sympathy ("If two people are in love, why shouldn't they be able to make a lifelong commitment to each other? How cruel to prevent those who love each other, even if they are of the same gender, from being able to express their love in the permanence of marriage.")
- *Ridicule and name-calling.* Ridicule and name-calling are not good techniques to use in a persuasive essay. Instead of exploring the strengths of the topic, the writer who uses these relies on making those who oppose the main idea look foolish, evil, or stupid. In most cases, the writer who does this weakens the argument.
- *Bandwagon.* The writer who uses the bandwagon technique uses the idea that "Everybody thinks this or is doing this; therefore it is valid." The bandwagon method is not a very authoritative way to convince your reader of your point.

Words and Phrases Common to Persuasive Essays

accordingly
because
consequently
clearly
for this reason
this is why
indeed
it is necessary to
it makes sense to
it seems clear that
it stands to reason
it then follows that
obviously
since
subsequently
therefore
thus
we must

Children Benefit from Gay Marriage

Editor's Notes The first model essay argues that gay marriage is a positive development for children. The author explains why she believes gay couples are fit to be parents, and argues that allowing gay couples to marry only strengthens their ability to raise natural and adopted children. The essay is structured as a five-paragraph essay in which each paragraph contributes a supporting piece of evidence to develop the argument.

The notes in the margin point out key features of the essay, and will help you understand how the essay is organized. Also note that all sources are cited using Modern Language Association (MLA) style. For more information on how to cite your sources see Appendix C. In addition, consider the following:

- How does the introduction engage the reader's attention?
- What persuasive techniques used in the essay?
- What purpose do the essay's quotes serve?
- Does the essay convince you of its point?

Refers to thesis and topic sentences

Refers to supporting details

Paragraph 1

The author opens her essay with an anecdote, a related story meant to interest the reader in what the essay has to say.

Judith McMullin is a happy, healthy, twenty-nine year old living in Brooklyn, New York. In a stable, loving relationship, she is also an accomplished professional, with two advanced degrees under her belt and a challenging career in the nutrition industry. Yet some close-minded people might be surprised to learn that Judith was raised by gay parents. Not surprisingly, being raised by two dads did not turn Judith into a maladjusted freak, which some believe is the only possible outcome of gay parenting. On the contrary, gays

Editor's Note: In applying MLA style guidelines in this book, the following simplifications have been made: Parenthetical text citations are confined to direct quotations only; electronic source documentation in the Works Cited list omits date of access, page ranges, and some detailed facts of publication.

make excellent parents, and should be granted the right to marry for the sake of children everywhere.

Paragraph 2

Gays can make fine parents, as millions of American children have learned. According to the 2000 census, one quarter of all same-sex-couple households included children, and more than one million American children are currently being raised by gay parents. And are they being treated any better or worse than the children of straight parents? Not likely. In 1995 the American Psychological Association found that children raised by gay parents are not disadvantaged in any significant way compared with children of straight parents. Three subsequent studies by other organizations, including the American Academy of Child and Adolescent Psychiatry and the American Academy of Pediatrics, confirmed these results. E.J. Graff, the author of *What is Marriage For? The Strange Social History of Our Most Intimate Institution* further confirms that children are not disadvantaged by being raised in gay households. "More than 20 studies have been done on about 300 children of lesbians and gay men. ... The results are quite clear: Children of lesbian or gay parents turn out just fine on every conceivable measure of emotional and social development." (Graff) Gays can, and do, make fine parents, and arguments against their parenting abilities are baseless and ignorant.

Paragraph 3

Secondly, extending marriage rights to gay couples would provide stable two-parent homes to countless adoptable children. Infants through teenagers have been neglected, abused, or abandoned by their birth parents, and are in need of loving homes; gay couples can and want to be there for them. But even adopting children is a challenge for gay couples; while Florida is the only state that actually bars gay couples from adopting, other states put up so many financial and bureaucratic obstacles for gay couples that adoption becomes nearly impossible. Allowing gays to marry,

This is the essay's thesis statement—it tells the reader what point the author is trying to convince you of.

This is the topic sentence of paragraph 2. It tells what this paragraph will focus on.

This information was taken from Viewpoint 5. Remember to store useful information that can be used to support your arguments.

Why has the author included the title of E.J. Graff's book before the quotation? What does this information tell you about Graff?

This is the topic sentence of paragraph three.

however, would likely surmount many of these obstacles, benefiting both gay couples who want to be parents and the millions of children that need them. "These children need strong statutes that let co-moms and co-dads adopt—preferably without the intrusive home study, the thousands of dollars in legal fees, and the reference letters from colleagues and friends that are now required." (Graff). It is inherently unfair that gay couples should be so painfully scrutinized by adoption councils—the courts, after all, do not come barging down the doors of derelicts and dead-beat dads, checking on their qualifications to make children. The insinuation that sexual orientation makes a person less fit to love and nurture a child is all the more ridiculous when one considers the millions of terrible parents who, by accident, happen to be straight.

Paragraph 4

Finally, since gays find ways to be parents anyway, better to have their natural or adopted children be raised under the umbrella of marriage than not. Surely no one can debate that marriage is a preferable environment for children; this is why divorce is typically eschewed by society, because it leaves a trail of broken homes and children who lose their sense of trust and safety. In addition, households with two parents run more smoothly and with more income than households with one. So if marriage is a preferable environment for children, wouldn't it be advantageous to provide the children of same-sex couples with as secure and stable an environment as possible—i.e., by allowing their parents to become married? As Dale Carpenter writes, "If it's better for children to be raised by a married opposite-sex couple than by an unmarried opposite-sex couple, it would surely be better for children to be raised by a married same-sex couple than by an unmarried same-sex couple."

Paragraph 5

As Judith McMullin and countless other people who have been raised by gay parents can attest, extending the institution of marriage to gay couples and their children can only be a positive thing—for families and society at large. In both straight and gay households, marriage can help parents and children acquire love and stability, and learn the important values of commitment and trust. For these reasons, America should legalize gay marriage. Many of those opposed to gay marriage claim to have the best concerns of children at heart; how short-sighted, then, that they oppose legalizing the very institution that could truly benefit children.

The conclusion comes back to the initial anecdote laid down in the introduction.

Did the author convince you that gay marriage helps children? Why or why not? What points or pieces of evidence did you find most convincing? What about least convincing?

Works Cited

Carpenter, Dale. "Gay Marriage Helps Children." *Independent Gay Forum* 1 Apr. 2004.

Graff, E.J. "The Other Marriage War: There's One Group that is Pursuing Legal Union, and Its Kids Need the Stability." *American Prospect* Vol. 13 8 Apr. 2002.

Exercise 1A: Create an Outline from an Existing Essay

It often helps to create an outline of the five-paragraph essay before you write it. The outline can help you organize the information, arguments, and evidence you have gathered during your research.

For this exercise, create an outline that could have been used to write Model Essay 1, *Children Benefit from Gay Marriage*. This "reverse engineering" exercise is meant to help familiarize you with how outlines can help classify and arrange information.

To do this you will need to
1. articulate the essay's thesis
2. pinpoint important pieces of evidence
3. flag quotes that supported the essay's ideas, and
4. identify key points that supported the argument.

Part of the outline has already been started to give you an idea of the assignment.

Outline

I. **Paragraph One**

A. Write the essay's thesis:

II. **Paragraph Two**

Topic: Gay couples make good parents.

A.

B. Quote from E.J. Graff arguing that studies show that children raised in gay households are not different from children raised in straight households.

III. Paragraph Three

Topic:

A. Many children need stable, loving homes that gay parents, if married, could provide.

B.

IV. Paragraph Four

Topic:

A. Households with two parents run more smoothly and with more income than households with one.

B. If marriage is a preferable environment for children, it makes sense to provide the children of same-sex couples with married parents.

V. Paragraph Five

A. Write the essay's conclusion:

Exercise 1B: Identifying Persuasive Techniques

Essayists use many techniques to persuade you to agree with their ideas or to do something they want you to do. Some of the most common techniques are described in Preface B of this section, "The Persuasive Essay." These tools are facts and statistics, opinions, testimonials, examples and anecdotes, appeals to reason, appeals to emotion, ridicule and name-calling, and bandwagon. Go back to the preface and review these tools. Remember that most of these tools can be used to enhance your essay, but some of them—particularly ridiculing, name-calling, and bandwagon—can detract from the essay's effectiveness. Nevertheless, you should be able to recognize them in the essays you read.

Some writers use one persuasive tool throughout their whole essay. For example, the essay may be one extended anecdote, or the writer may rely entirely on statistics. But most writers typically use a combination of persuasive tools. Model Essay 1, "Children Benefit from Gay Marriage," does this. The sidebar notes point out some of the persuasive tools used in the essay.

Read Model Essay 1 again and see if you can find every persuasive tool used. Put that information in the following table. Part of the table is filled in for you. Explanatory notes are underneath the table. (NOTE: You will not fill in every box. No paragraph contains all of the techniques.)

	Paragraph 1 Sentence #	Paragraph 2 Sentence #	Paragraph 3 Sentence #	Paragraph 4 Sentence #	Paragraph 5 Sentence #
Fact			3[a]		
Statistic		2[b]			
Opinion			6[c]		
Testimonial					
Example					
Anecdote					
Appeal to Reason			1[d]		
Appeal to Emotion					
Ridicule					
Name-Calling					
Bandwagon				2[e]	

NOTES

a. That Florida is the only state to prohibit gays from adopting is a fact.

b. This figure about children being raised in gay households taken from the U.S. census is a statistic.

c. It is the author's opinion that this is "inherently" unfair.

d. The author is attempting to appeal to the reader's sense of logic and reason. Since gays are going to have children anyway, she reasons, better to have them do it under the umbrella of marriage than not.

e. "No one can debate" is a bandwagon technique—the author is trying to appear as if everyone agrees with her perspective, and thus you should too.

Now, look at the table you have produced. Which persuasive tools does this essay rely on most heavily? Which are not used at all?

Apply this exercise to the other model essays in this section when you are finished reading them.

What Does Your Marriage Have to Do With Mine, Exactly? Why Gay Marriage Does Not Threaten the Institution of Marriage

Editor's Notes The second model essay argues that gay marriage does not threaten the institution of marriage, as many of its opponents have claimed. The author argues that gay marriage has no bearing on other peoples' personal relationships and strengthens society by including more people in the society-stabilizing institution. The essay is structured as a five-paragraph essay in which each paragraph contributes a supporting piece of evidence to develop the argument.

As you read this essay, take note of its components and how they are organized (the sidebars in the margins provide further explanation).

■ Refers to thesis and topic sentences

■ Refers to supporting details

Paragraph 1

In the furious debate over gay marriage, one argument has cropped up repeatedly which never quite makes sense: The charge made by many conservatives, including President George W. Bush, that were homosexuals to marry, it would threaten the institution of marriage. On the surface, the fear seems palpable—marriage is an important thing, often credited as the building block of our entire civilization. Any threat to this foundational institution should be taken seriously. But, thinking more critically on the matter, it seems most improbable that gay marriage could have any effect, negative or positive, on straight marriages.

What is the essay's thesis statement? How did you recognize it?

Paragraph 2

The most basic reason why gay marriage does not threaten straight marriage is that marriages are not dependent on one another. The status of the Jones's relationship has nothing to do with that of their neighbors, the Smiths. Claims that

What is the topic sentence of paragraph 2?

73

gay marriage somehow threatens the sanctity of marriages between men and women are bogeyman arguments meant to scare ignorant Americans into thinking that somehow their marriage will be in trouble. "I am in the 54th year of a happy marriage," writes one straight man who favors gay marriage. "I do not feel that my marriage is threatened by expanding the meaning of the word 'marriage.' No one is invading my home or kidnapping my wife or children. Nor is the institution of marriage threatened. That people of the same sex might unite in a bond of trust is a far less serious threat to the institution of marriage than the need for both partners to hold down full-time jobs." (Stein) In the same way that individual heterosexual marriages have no bearing on the quality of other heterosexual marriages, neither would gay marriages.

What point does this quote support? What does it offer that the author of the essay cannot say for herself?

Paragraph 3

What is the topic sentence of paragraph 3?

In truth, if heterosexuals are worried about threats to the institution of marriage, they should look inward for the source of the problem. The Associated Press reports that 22 percent of all married men and 14 percent of married women have had at least one affair during their marriage. In modern times, more than half of all marriages end in divorce, and the Centers for Disease Control and Prevention has found that 43 percent of first marriages end in separation or divorce within the first 15 years. Such statistics indicate that heterosexual couples have done a great job of threatening marriage all on their own.

How do these statistics directly support the paragraph's topic?

Paragraph 4

What is the topic sentence of paragraph 4? How is it different from the other topics that have been put forth? In what way does it support the essay's thesis?

Finally, marriage faces a multitude of threats, many of which are more serious than gay marriage could ever present. We live in an age of "Xtreme marriages" where it is common for celebrities to have four, even five marriages, some of which last mere hours (such as the infamous 55-hour marriage of Britney Spears to a childhood friend in 2004). The marriages of some of the most esteemed members of our society—religious leaders, politicians, even the president himself—have faced threats, none of which have had anything to do with homosexuals. As one journalist writes, "Plenty of things do threaten traditional marriage: substance abuse, selfishness, greed, low self-esteem, financial struggles, depression, unrealistic expectations, domestic abuse, poor role models, the media and its hyper-focus on youth and sex, Internet pornography and chat rooms and more." (Paolino) The heterosexual community needs to address these pressing threats to marriage before they start lambasting homosexuals for their supposed ruinous effects on the institution.

> What transitions are used to keep the essay moving? Make a list of all transitional words and phrases that appear.

Paragraph 5

Calling gay marriage a threat to the institution of marriage is nothing more than discriminatory scapegoating. Put simply, it represents homophobia at its worst. A marriage between Mary and Lisa will have no bearing on a marriage between James and Tiffany. To find threats in homosexual relationships is to obfuscate the problems that heterosexual relationships have all on their own. As journalist Tammy Paolino argues, "Before we begin blaming committed gay couples for dismantling the institution of marriage, maybe we should look around and take stock of what we ourselves are doing to protect it in the first place."

> Note how the conclusion brings the essay to a close without repeating the points that were made in the essay.

Works Cited

Paolino, Tammy. "Gays Don't Threaten 'Tradition' of Marriage." *Courier-Post* 18 Jan 2004.

Stein, Sherman. "Marriage Can Be Expanded." *Los Angeles Times* 5 June 2004.

Exercise 2A: Create an Outline from an Existing Essay

As you did for the first model essay in this section, create an outline that could have been used to write "What Does Your Marriage Have to Do with Mine, Exactly? Why Gay Marriage Does Not Threaten the Institution of Marriage." Be sure to identify the essay's thesis statement, its supporting ideas, its descriptive passages, and key pieces of evidence that were used.

Exercise 2B: Create an Outline for Your Own Essay

The second model essay expresses a particular point of view about gay marriage. For this exercise, your assignment is to find supporting ideas, choose specific and concrete details, create an outline, and ultimately write a five-paragraph essay making a different, or even opposing, point about gay marriage. Your goal is to use persuasive techniques to convince your reader.

Step I: Write a Thesis Statement

The following thesis statement would be appropriate for an opposing essay on why gay marriage threatens the institution of marriage:

> The sacred institution of marriage, which has been a pillar of civilization for thousands of years, cannot endure the inclusion of people of the same sex, or even groups of people, without being damaged in an irrevocable way.

Or see the sample paper topics suggested in Appendix D for more ideas.

Step II: Brainstorm Pieces of Supporting Evidence

Using information from some of the viewpoints in the previous section and from the information found in Section III of this book, write down three arguments or pieces of evidence that support the thesis statement you selected. Then, for each of these three arguments, write down supportive facts, examples, and details that support it. These could be:

- statistical information
- personal memories and anecdotes
- quotes from experts, peers, or family members
- observations of people's actions and behaviors
- specific and concrete details

Supporting pieces of evidence for the above sample thesis statement are found in this book, and include:

- Quote from Charles Colson in Viewpoint 3: "Marriage is the traditional building block of human society, intended both to unite couples and bring children into the world. Tragically, the sexual revolution led to the decoupling of marriage and procreation; same-sex 'marriage' would pull them completely apart, leading to an explosive increase in family collapse, out-of-wedlock births and crime."
- Point made by James Phelan in Viewpoint 2 that marriage is already burdened, and the violence, instability, health issues, and infidelity that he claims gay marriages will add to the institution will damage it further.
- Quote box in Viewpoint 6 from Sharon Slater: "Once we abandon marriage to the whims and desires of adults seeking validation of their sexual lifestyles, we denigrate children and their needs—legally validating relationships that would deliberately leave them motherless or fatherless. And that hurts society."

Step III: Place the information from Step I in outline form.

Step IV: Write the arguments or supporting statements in paragraph form.

By now you have three arguments that support the essay's thesis statement, as well as supporting material. Use the outline to write out your three supporting arguments in paragraph form. Make sure each paragraph has a topic sentence that states the paragraph's thesis clearly and broadly. Then add supporting sentences that express the facts, quotes, details, and examples that support the paragraph's argument. The paragraph may also have a concluding or summary sentence.

The Slippery Slope of Gay Marriage

Editor's Notes The final model essay argues against gay marriage, suggesting it will send society down a slippery slope of immorality and chaos. It is different from the other two model essays you have read in that it opposes gay marriage and tries to persuade you that you should too.

This essay also differs from the previous model essays in that it is longer than five paragraphs. Sometimes five paragraphs are simply not enough to adequately develop an idea. Extending the length of an essay can allow the reader to explore a topic in more depth or present multiple pieces of evidence that together provide a complete picture of a topic. Longer essays can also help readers discover the complexity of a subject by examining a topic beyond its superficial exterior. Moreover, the ability to write a sustained research or position paper is a valuable skill you will need as you advance academically.

As you read, consider the questions posed in the margins. Continue to identify thesis statements, supporting details, transitions, and quotations. Examine the introductory and concluding paragraphs to understand how they give shape to the essay. Finally, evaluate the essay's general structure and assess its overall effectiveness.

■ Refers to thesis and topic sentences

■ Refers to supporting details

Paragraph 1

One of the most often-heard battle cries in the war over whether homosexuals should be granted the right to marry is that gay marriages don't hurt anyone else; they only enhance the joy of the people in the relationship. The truth of the matter, however, is that gay marriages *do* hurt people outside the relationship. They endanger the institution of marriage, they endanger children raised in that marriage,

What is the essay's thesis statement? How did you recognize it?

79

and they threaten to send society down a slippery slope towards chaos and immorality. We cannot afford to allow the selfish desires of individuals trump the greater good of society.

Paragraph 2

What is the topic sentence of paragraph 2?

Marriage cannot be extended to homosexual couples simply because the very definition of marriage is a union between a man and a woman. Marriage has existed for thousands of years for one important purpose: to create and raise children in a nurturing environment. Homosexuals cannot naturally have children; what reason, then, is there for their marriage? As analyst Stanley Kurtz writes, "It follows that once marriage is redefined to accommodate same sex couples, that change cannot help but lock in and reinforce the very cultural separation between marriage and parenthood that makes gay marriage conceivable to begin with." (qtd. in Colson, 72). Extending marriage to homosexuals is a violation of what the institution is for, and on these grounds should be rejected.

Paragraph 3

Note that these are the same statistics used in model essay two—yet here they are used to support a completely different argument! This is an important feature of statistics—they don't mean much until they are put in context.

Allowing gays to marry would put much strain on an already troubled institution. Indeed, modern marriage is in severe jeopardy: The Associated Press reports that 22 percent of all married men and 14 percent of married women have had at least one affair during their marriage. In modern times, more than half of all marriages end in divorce, and the Centers for Disease Control and Prevention has found that 43 percent of first marriages end in separation or divorce within the first 15 years. Marriage has further suffered under the strains of the necessity for two incomes; the increase in domestic abuse and substance abuse, and the perverse temptations of the Internet. Indeed, marriage in the 21st century is a struggling and frail institution.

Paragraph 4

Adding gay couples to the mix—which bring to the table their own issues of infidelity, substance abuse, and commitment—would be the final nail in the coffin of our most sacred foundational building block. According to the Male Couple, a project that studies the nature of homosexual relationships, gay relationships tend to end faster than straight relationships. Of 156 couples studied, only 7 maintained fidelity. On the whole, the project found the average length of homosexual relationships is just 2 years. Says one social worker, "Given their history, 'gay' men will not stay in monogamous relationships and therefore are not good candidates for marriage." (Phelan, 21)

> What pieces of evidence support this paragraph's topic?

> This quote was taken from Viewpoint 2. Note how it supports the essay's topic.

Paragraph 5

In addition to not being good candidates for marriage, the advent of gay marriage would likely lead to an increased number of children raised in gay households, which can hold no good for our culture. Society has already witnessed the effect being raised without both a mother and father has had on our world. In the twentieth century, divorces became more common than ever before, and this was accompanied in a rise of crime, imprisonment, drug use, and violence. According to Charles Colson, who runs Prison Fellowship Ministries, a religious-based and criminal justice reform organization, boys who grow up without their fathers are twice as likely to end up in prison as boys who grow up with both parents present. Similarly, sixty percent of rapists and 72 percent of teenage murderers grew up without their fathers present in their lives. We can only imagine the consequences of purposely allowing children to be raised by only one gender. Yes, children raised by homosexual parents will have the benefit of having two people present, unlike single-parent households from which children tend to emerge troubled. But two men or two women cannot compensate for the critical qualities both genders contribute to a child's development.

> What is the topic of paragraph 5?

> What transitions are used in the essay? Make a list of all that appear.

What is the topic sentence of paragraph 6? How does it support the essay's thesis?

With more children missing the critical two-gender parent recipe during their childhood, it is very likely that crime and violence will increase. According to Colson, 90 percent of kids from broken families get into trouble, while just 10 percent of kids from intact families do. From such grim statistics, no one can argue that it is likely that the children of gay and lesbian couples will be more prone be involved with drugs, crime, violence, etc. As Colson writes, "If we fail to enact a Federal Marriage Amendment [that would define marriage as being between a man and a woman], we can expect, not just more family breakdown, but also more criminals behind bars and more chaos in our streets." (Colson, 72) Such instability will strain all of society, which already cannot manage the growing numbers of disengaged youth and the disturbance they wreak on our social systems.

What authority does Colson have to speak on the subject?

Make a list of the persuasive techniques used in this essay. Do you find facts and statistics? What about testimonials and anecdotes? Appeals to reason? Emotion? Efforts to ridicule or to jump on the bandwagon? Complete the chart found in Exercise 1B using this essay.

A final consequence of gay marriage is that it will send society down a slippery slope, creating a precedent for allowing blasphemous unions between groups of people (known as polygamy or polyamory), or even unions between humans and animals. It is hard to see how legalizing same-sex marriage will not eventually lead to such arrangements—if the definition of marriage is changed so that it no longer states that marriage is between one man and one woman, there is nothing preventing marriage from including a wide range of combinations, human and otherwise. Permitting anything other than heterosexual marriage sends society on a "slippery slope," down which it will tumble until there is nothing left of the institution of marriage. As Timothy Dailey of the Family Research Council has put it, "Once marriage is no longer confined to a man and a woman, it is impossible to exclude virtually any relationship between two or more partners of either sex—even non-human 'partners.'" Therefore, same-sex marriage must be resisted and marriage must be defined as that which is between a man and a woman.

Paragraph 8

Presented here are just a few of the ways in which gay marriage threatens to send society into upheaval. Gay marriage is good for no one but the homosexual couples who want the rest of the world to see their relationships as legitimate. Fortunately, there are those of us who are looking out not just for the individual happiness of a few, but the greater good of us all.

How does the conclusion return to the ideas put forth in the introduction?

Works Cited

Colson, Charles. "Societal Suicide." *Christianity Today* June 2004: 72.

Dailey, Timothy J. "The Slippery Slope of Same-Sex 'Marriage.'" Brochure published by the Family Research Council (available online at www.frc.org).

Phelan, James. "Why Not 'Gay' Marriage in Canada?" *Catholic Insight* May 2005: 18–21.

Every essay features introductory and concluding paragraphs that are used to frame the main ideas being presented. Along with presenting the essay's thesis statement, well-written introductions should grab the attention of the reader and make clear why the topic being explored is important. The conclusion reiterates the essay's thesis and is also the last chance for the writer to make an impression on the reader. Strong introductions and conclusions can greatly enhance an essay's effect on an audience.

The Introduction

There are several techniques that can be used to craft an introductory paragraph. An essay can start with:

- an anecdote: a brief story that illustrates a point relevant to the topic.
- startling information: facts or statistics that elucidate the point of the essay.
- setting up and knocking down a position: a position or claim believed by proponents of one side of a controversy, followed by statements that challenge that claim.
- historical perspective: an example of the way things used to be that leads into a discussion of how or why things work differently now.
- summary information: general introductory information about the topic that feeds into the essay's thesis statement.

Problem One
Reread the introductory paragraphs of the model essays and of the viewpoints in Section I. Identify which of the techniques described above are used in the example essays. How do they grab the attention of the reader? Are their thesis statements clearly presented?

Problem Two

Write an introduction for the essay you have outlined and partially written in Exercise 2B using one of the techniques described above.

The Conclusion

The conclusion brings the essay to a close by summarizing or returning to its main ideas. Good conclusions, however, go beyond simply repeating these ideas. Strong conclusions explore a topic's broader implications and reiterate why it is important for the reader to consider. Conclusions may frame the essay by returning to an anecdote featured in the opening paragraph. Or they may close with a quotation or refer back to an event in the essay. In opinionated essays, the conclusion can reiterate the side the essay is taking or ask the reader to reconsider a previously held position on the subject.

Problem Three

Reread the concluding paragraphs of the model essays and of the viewpoints in Section I. Which were most effective in driving their arguments home to the reader? What sorts of techniques did they use to do this? Did they appeal emotionally to the reader, or bookend an idea or event referenced elsewhere in the essay?

Problem Four

Write a conclusion for the essay you have outlined and partially written in Exercise 2B using one of the techniques described above.

Exercise 3B: Using Quotations to Enliven Your Essay

No essay is complete without quotations. Get in the habit of using quotes to support at least some of the ideas in your essays. Quotes do not need to appear in every paragraph, but they should appear often enough so that the essay contains voices aside from your own. When you write, use quotations to accomplish the following:

- Provide expert advice that you are not necessarily in the position to know about.
- Cite lively or passionate passages.
- Include a particularly well-written point that gets to the heart of the matter.
- Supply statistics or facts that have been derived from someone's research.
- Deliver anecdotes that illustrate the point you are trying to make.
- Express first-person testimony.

Problem One: Reread the essays presented in all sections of this book and find at least one example of each of the above quotation types.

There are a couple of important things to remember when using quotations.

- Note your sources' qualifications and biases. This way your reader can identify the person you have quoted and can put their words in a context.
- Put any quoted material within proper quotation marks. Failing to attribute quotes to their authors constitutes plagiarism, which is when an author takes someone else's words or ideas and presents them as their own. Plagiarism is a form of intellectual theft and must be avoided at all costs.

Write Your Own Persuasive Five-Paragraph Essay

Using the information from this book, write your own five-paragraph persuasive essay that deals with gay marriage. You can use the resources in this book for information about issues relating to this topic and how to structure this type of essay.

The following steps are suggestions on how to get started.

Step One: Choose your topic.

The first step is to decide what topic to write your persuasive essay on. Is there any subject that particularly fascinates you? Is there an issue you strongly support, or feel strongly against? Is there a topic you feel personally connected to or one that you would like to learn more about? Ask yourself such questions before selecting your essay topic. Refer to Appendix D: Sample Essay Topics if you need help selecting a topic.

Step Two: Write down questions and answers about the topic.

Before you begin writing, you will need to think carefully about what ideas your essay will contain. This is a process known as *brainstorming*. Brainstorming involves asking yourself questions and coming up with ideas to discuss in your essay. Possible questions that will help you with the brainstorming process include:

- Why is this topic important?
- Why should people be interested in this topic?
- How can I make this essay interesting to the reader?
- What question am I going to address in this paragraph or essay?
- What facts, ideas, or quotes can I use to support the answer to my question?

Step Three: Gather facts, ideas, and anecdotes related to your topic.

This book contains several places to find information, including the viewpoints and the appendices. In addition, you may want to research the books, articles, and Web sites listed in Section III, or do additional research in your local library. You can also conduct interviews if you know someone who has a compelling story that would fit well in your essay.

Step Four: Develop a workable thesis statement.

Use what you have written down in steps two and three to help you articulate the main point or argument you want to make in your essay. It should be expressed in a clear sentence and make an arguable or supportable point.

Example:

> *Because the American public is more likely to favor civil unions for gay couples, the homosexual community should push for civil union rights before they try and normalize the concept of homosexual marriage.*

(This could be the thesis statement of a persuasive essay that argues that since homosexuals have a better chance of getting civil union rights than marriage rights, they should put their efforts towards achieving those rights, and seek marriage rights after the general public becomes more comfortable with the idea of institutionalized homosexual relationships.)

Step Five: Write an outline or diagram.
   a. Write the thesis statement at the top of the outline.
   b. Write roman numerals I, II, and III on the left side of the page.
   c. Next to each Roman numeral, write down the best ideas you came up with in step three. These should all directly relate to and support the thesis statement.
   d. Next to each letter write down information that supports that particular idea.

Step Six: Write the three supporting paragraphs.
Use your outline to write the three supporting paragraphs. Write down the main idea of each paragraph in sentence form. Do the same thing for the supporting points of information. Each sentence should support the paragraph of the topic. Be sure you have relevant and interesting details, facts, and quotes. Use transitions when you move from idea to idea to keep the text fluid and smooth. Sometimes, although not always, paragraphs can include a concluding or summary sentence that restates the paragraph's argument.

Step Seven: Write the introduction and conclusion.
See Exercise 3A for information on writing introductions and conclusions.

Step Eight: Read and rewrite.
As you read, check your essay for the following:
- ✔ Does the essay maintain a consistent tone?
- ✔ Do all paragraphs reinforce your general thesis?
- ✔ Do all paragraphs flow from one to the other? Do you need to add transition words or phrases?
- ✔ Have you quoted from reliable, authoritative, and interesting sources?
- ✔ Is there a sense of progression throughout the essay?
- ✔ Does the essay get bogged down in too much detail or irrelevant material?
- ✔ Does your introduction grab the reader's attention?
- ✔ Does your conclusion reflect back on any previously discussed material, or give the essay a sense of closure?
- ✔ Are there any spelling or grammatical errors?

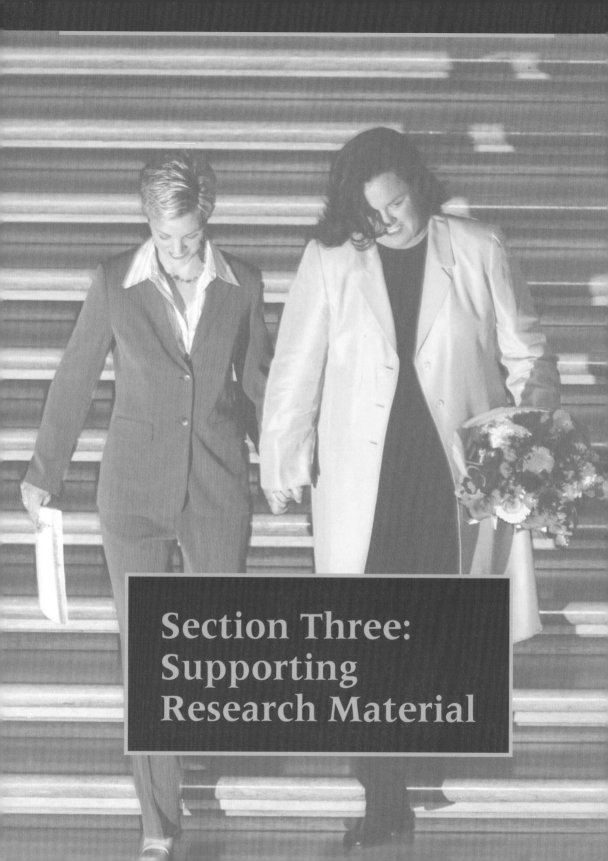

Section Three:
Supporting
Research Material

Facts About Gay Marriage

Editor's Note: These facts can be used in reports or papers to reinforce or add credibility when making important points or claims.

Gay Marriage around the World

- The Netherlands became the first country in the world to legalize same-sex marriages on April 1, 2001.
- Belgium followed in 2003.
- In 2005, Spain and Canada legalized gay marriage, followed by South Africa in 2006.
- According to United Press International, less than 10 percent of the 50,000 estimated same-sex couples in the Netherlands have opted to marry.
- Denmark, Sweden, Norway, Finland, and Iceland grant same-sex couples the same rights as heterosexual couples.
- Argentina, Canada, Hungary, France, Portugal, Britain, and Germany grant some form of civil unions to same-sex couples.
- Italy and Spain are two of the many countries around the world that do not legally recognize same-sex relationships.
- Some Swiss cities, such as Zurich and Geneva, provide certain legal rights to same-sex couples.

According to the International Gay & Lesbian Human Rights Commission:

- Homosexual acts are illegal in many countries, including Afghanistan, Algeria, Barbados, Botswana, Cameroon, Ethiopia, Georgia, India, Iran, Kenya, Malaysia, Morocco, Nepal, Nicaragua, Sri Lanka, Syria, and Zimbabwe.

- Some of these nations punish homosexual acts with the death penalty or life in prison. In Iran, those found guilty of homosexuality can be put to death in one of four ways: being hanged, stoned, pierced with a sword, or dropped from a high place.
- In Botswana, sex between two men is punishable with up to 7 years in prison, while in India, perpetrators can be sentenced to up to life in prison.

Gay Marriage in the United States

- Massachusetts is the only state to allow legalized marriage. Gay couples have been able to legally wed there since 2003, and thousands have done so.
- In February 2004, the city of San Francisco began granting marriage licenses to same-sex couples. People traveled from all around the country to obtain a legal marriage license, which were not recognized by their home states.
- Nearly 4,000 same-sex couples obtained marriage licenses in San Francisco in the four weeks before the California state Supreme Court halted the process in August 2004.
- In the 2004 and 2006 elections, voters in 26 states elected to adopt amendments that clarify marriage as between a man and a woman. Those states are: Alabama, Alaska, Arkansas, Colorado, Georgia, Hawaii, Idaho, Kansas, Kentucky, Louisiana, Michigan, Mississippi, Missouri, Montana, Nebraska, Nevada, North Dakota, Ohio, Oklahoma, Oregon, South Carolina, South Dakota, Tennessee, Texas, Utah, Virginia, and Wisconsin.
- The proposal to amend the constitution to ban gay marriage was rare in that amendments to the Constitution typically expand the rights of Americans. The only other time that the Constitution was amended to specifically ban something was in 1920, when for 13 years the production and consumption of alcoholic beverages was federally prohibited.

- Civil unions provide gay couples with the same rights and benefits that married people have, including hospital visitation rights, access to medical information, survivor benefits, spousal military benefits, adoption rights, and many others.
- Civil unions are legal in Connecticut, New Jersey and Vermont.
- Marriage laws tend to be left to the states. The US Supreme Court has interfered in state laws regarding marriage just twice—to require Utah to ban the practice of polygamy in the nineteenth century, and to force 16 states to legalize interracial marriage in 1967.

The Institution of Marriage in America
- According to the Centers for Disease Control, 43 percent of first marriages end in separation or divorce within 15 years.
- The Associated Press reports that about 22 percent of all married men and 14 percent of all married women have had at least one affair during their marriage.
- There are approximately 50,000 to 60,000 polygamists in the United States.
- The U.S. has one of the highest divorce rates in the world, ranking 12th on the list of divorce rates by country, according to *Divorce Magazine*.
- Ranking ahead of the U.S. are Belarus (68 percent of marriages there end in divorce), Russia (65 percent), Sweden (64 percent), Latvia (63 percent), Ukraine (63 percent), Czech Republic (61 percent), Belgium (56 percent), Finland (56 percent), Lithuania (55 percent), United Kingdom (53 percent), Moldova (52 percent), and then the United States (49 percent).
- The countries with the lowest divorce rates include: Tajikistan (13 percent), Georgia (12 percent), Italy (12 percent), Uzbekistan (12 percent), Albania (7 percent), Turkey (6 percent).
- Macedonia has the lowest divorce rate in the world, at 5 percent.

Marriage's Effect on Children

- According to *Christianity Today*, girls who are raised without a father in the home are five times more likely to become pregnant as a teen, while boys who are raised without a father in the home are twice as likely to end up in prison.
- In 1995, the American Psychological Association found that children raised by gay parents are not disadvantaged in any significant way compared to the children of heterosexual parents. Three subsequent studies by other organizations, such as the American Academy of Child and Adolescent Psychiatry and the American Academy of Pediatrics, confirmed these results.
- The American Academy of Pediatrics' Committee on Psychosocial Aspects of Child and Family Health issued a report in 2002—the most recent comprehensive review of gay-parenting studies. It found no meaningful differences between children raised by gay parents and those raised by heterosexual parents.
- Just 10 states specifically allow gay and lesbian couples to adopt kids: California, Connecticut, Illinois, New Jersey, New York, Pennsylvania, Massachusetts, Vermont, Washington, and Wisconsin.
- Florida is the only state that prohibits gay couples from adopting children.
- There are approximately 10 million children in the United States who have at least one parent who is gay or lesbian.

According to the 2000 U.S. census:

- Across the country there are over 1 million children being raised by gay parents.
- One quarter of the homosexual households in America contain children.
- In California, half of married couples and one-third of gay couples are raising children.

- More than 70,000 children in California are being raised by gay couples.
- According to Urban Institute, a social research organization, 96 percent of all U.S. counties have at least one same-sex couple raising children.

American Opinions on Gay Marriage

- Younger people are more likely to support gay marriage. According to *The Economist,* just 21 percent of those over 65 support gay marriage, while 55 percent of 18- to 29-year-olds do.
- According to a Harris poll taken in March 2004, 71 percent of all gay, lesbian and bisexual people surveyed said that gay couples should be allowed to marry.
- One in three Californians supports gay marriage, according to a 2004 *Los Angeles Times* poll.
- According to a Harris poll taken in March 2004, 47 percent of Americans believed that denying same-sex couples the right to marry was not a violation of the principle that all people should be treated equally.
- According to an April 2005 CNN/USA Today/Gallup poll, 68 percent of Americans believed that same-sex marriages should not be recognized as valid; 28 percent said they should be recognized as valid, while 4 percent had no opinion.

Finding and Using Sources of Information

No matter what type of essay you are writing, it is necessary to find information to support your point of view. You can use sources such as books, magazine articles, newspaper articles, and online articles.

Using Books and Articles

You can find books and articles in a library by using the library's computer or cataloging system. If you are not sure how to use these resources, ask a librarian to help you. You can also use a computer to find many magazine articles and other articles written specifically for the Internet.

You are likely to find a lot more information than you can possibly use in your essay, so your first task is to narrow it down to what is likely to be most usable. Look at book and article titles. Look at book chapter titles, and examine the book's index to see if it contains information on the specific topic you want to write about. (For example, if you want to write about civil unions and you find a book about gay marriage, check the chapter titles and index to be sure it contains information about civil unions before you bother to check out the book.)

For a five–paragraph essay, you do not need a great deal of supporting information, so quickly try to narrow down your materials to a few good books and magazine or Internet articles. You do not need dozens. You might even find that one or two good books or articles contain all the information you need.

You probably do not have time to read an entire book, so find the chapters or sections that relate to your topic, and skim these. When you find useful information, copy it onto a note card or notebook. You should look for supporting facts, statistics, quotations, and examples.

Using the Internet

When you select your supporting information, it is important that you evaluate its sources. This is especially important with information you find on the Internet. Because nearly anyone can put information on the Internet, there is as much bad information as good information. Before using Internet information—or any information—try to determine if the source seems to be reliable. Is the author or Internet site sponsored by a legitimate organization? Is it from a government source? Does the author have any special knowledge or training relating to the topic you are looking up? Does the article give any indication of where its information comes from?

Using Your Supporting Information

When you use supporting information from a book, article, interview or other source, there are three important things to remember:

1. *Make it clear whether you are using a direct quotation or a paraphrase.* If you copy information directly from your source, you are quoting it. You must put quotation marks around the information, and tell where the information comes from. If you put the information in your own words, you are paraphrasing it.

Here is an example of a using a quotation:
>   Author Stanley Kurtz believes that gay marriage threatens to swell society's understanding of marriage beyond a man and a woman, beyond two people, even: to groups of people, or even animals. Fears Kurtz: "Among the likeliest effects of gay marriage is to take us down a slippery slope to legalized polygamy and 'polyamory' (group marriage). Marriage will be transformed into a variety of relationship

contracts, linking two, three, or more individuals (however weakly and temporarily) in every conceivable combination of male and female."

Here is an example of a brief paraphrase of the same passage:

Author Stanley Kurtz believes that gay marriage threatens to swell society's understanding of marriage beyond a man and a woman, beyond two people, even: to groups of people, or even animals. Indeed, allowing gays to marry could send us down a slippery slope in which there is nothing to stop groups of people from wedding, no matter the superficiality of their commitment.

2. *Use the information fairly.* Be careful to use supporting information in the way the author intended it. For example, it is unfair to quote an author as saying, "Gay marriage threatens the institution of marriage" when he or she intended to say, "Gay marriage threatens the institution of marriage as much as walking around a cancer ward puts a person at risk of catching cancer." This is called taking information out of context. This is using supporting evidence unfairly.

3. *Give credit where credit is due.* Giving credit is known as citing. You must use citations when you use someone else's information, but not every piece of supporting information needs a citation.

   - If the supporting information is general knowledge—that is, it can be found in many sources—you do not have to cite your source.
   - If you directly quote a source, you must cite it.
   - If you paraphrase information from a specific source, you must cite it.

If you do not use citations where you should, you are plagiarizing—or stealing—someone else's work.

Citing Your Sources

There are a number of ways to cite your sources. Your teacher will probably want you to do it in one of three ways:

- Informal: As in the example in number 1 above, tell where you got the information as you present it in the text of your essay.

- Informal list: At the end of your essay, place an unnumbered list of all the sources you used. This tells the reader where, in general, your information came from.

- Formal: Use numbered footnotes. Footnotes are generally placed at the end of an article or essay, although they may be placed elsewhere depending on your teacher's requirements.

[...] ge." *Weekly Standard,*

Using MLA Style to Create a Works Cited List

You will probably need to create a list of works cited for your paper. These include materials that you quoted from, relied heavily on, or consulted to write your paper. There are several different ways to structure these references. The following examples are based on Modern Language Association (MLA) style, one of the major citation styles used by writers.

Book Entries

For most book entries you will need the author's name, the book's title, where it was published, what company published it, and the year it was published. This information is usually found on the inside of the book. Variations on book entries include the following:

A Book by a Single Author
> Guest, Emma. *Children of AIDS: Africa's Orphan Crisis.* London: Sterling, 2003.

Two or More Books by the Same Author
> Friedman, Thomas L. *The World Is Flat: A Brief History of the Twentieth Century.* New York: Farrar, Straus and Giroux, 2005.

> ---. *From Beirut to Jerusalem.* New York: Doubleday, 1989.

A Book by Two or More Authors
> Pojman, Louis P., and Jeffrey Reiman. *The Death Penalty: For and Against.* Lanham, MD: Rowman & Littlefield, 1998.

A Book with an Editor

Friedman, Lauri S., ed. *At Issue: What Motivates Suicide Bombers?* San Diego, CA: Greenhaven, 2004.

Periodical and Newspaper Entries

Entries for sources found in periodicals and newspapers are cited a bit differently than books. For one, these sources usually have a title and a publication name. They also may have specific dates and page numbers. Unlike book entries, you do not need to list where newspapers or periodicals are published or what company publishes them.

An Article from a Periodical
Snow, Keith Harmon. "State Terror in Ethiopia." *Z Magazine* June 2004: 33–35.

An Unsigned Article from a Periodical
"Broadcast Decency Rules." *Issues & Controversies on File* 30 April 2004.

An Article from a Newspaper
Constantino, Rebecca. "Fostering Love, Respecting Race." *Los Angeles Times* 14 December 2002: B17.

Internet Sources

To document a source you found online, try to provide as much information on it as possible, including the author's name, the title of the document, date of publication or of last revision, the URL, and your date of access.

A Web Source
Shyovitz, David. "The History and Development of Yiddish." Jewish Virtual Library. 30 May 2005 < http://www.jewishvirtuallibrary.org/jsource/ History/yiddish.html. > . Accessed September 11, 2007.

Your teacher will tell you exactly how information should be cited in your essay. Generally, the very least information needed is the original author's name and the name of the article or other publication.

Be sure you know exactly what information your teacher requires before you start looking for your supporting information so that you know what information to include with your notes.

Sample Essay Topics

The U.S. Should Adopt a Constitutional Amendment to Ban Gay Marriage

The U.S. Should Not Adopt a Constitutional Amendment to Ban Gay Marriage

Homosexual Couples Should Seek Civil Unions

All Marriages Should Be Dissolved to Civil Unions

The Gay Community Does Not Need the Guise of Marriage

The Government Should Legislate Moral Issues Moral Issues Such as Gay Marriage

The Government Should Not Legislate Moral Issues Such as Gay Marriage

The States Should Be Allowed to Decide Their Position on Gay Marriage

Prohibiting Gay Marriage Violates Civil Rights

Gay Marriage Is Not a Civil Rights Issue

Marriage Should Be Limited to a Man and a Woman

Marriage Should Be Extended to Any Loving Couple

Religious Definitions of Marriage Are Compatible with the State

Religious Definitions of Marriage Do Not Belong in the State

Gay Unions Threaten Society

Gay Unions Bolster Society

Gay Marriage Threaten the Institution of Marriage

Gay Marriage Does Not Threaten the Institution of Marriage

Gay Marriage Puts Society on a Slippery Slope by Encouraging Polygamy and Bestiality

Straight Couples Have Already Threatened the Institution of Marriage

Gay Marriage Would Hurt Children
Gay Marriage Would Help Children
Gay Couples Should Be Allowed to Adopt
Children Raised in Gay Households Are at Risk

Organizations to Contact

American Civil Liberties Union (ACLU)

132 W. 43rd St. New York, NY 10036 • (212) 944-9800 • Fax: (212) 359-5290 • Web site: www.aclu.org

The ACLU is the nation's oldest and largest civil liberties organization. Its Lesbian and Gay Rights/AIDS Project, started in 1986, handles litigation, education, and public policy work on behalf of gays and lesbians. The ACLU publishes the handbook *The Rights of Lesbians and Gay Men,* the briefing paper "Lesbian and Gay Rights," and the monthly newsletter *Civil Liberties Alert.*

American Family Communiversity (AFCO)

542 N. Artesian St., Chicago, IL 60612 • Phone and Fax: (312) 738-2207

AFCO is a multidisciplinary action and education agency engaged in upgrading the various policies, practices, procedures, professions, systems, and institutions affecting the stability and viability of marriage. It publishes the books *Divorce for the Unbroken Marriage* and *Therapeutic Family Law* as well as several monographs.

Canadian Lesbian and Gay Archives

Box 639, Station A, Toronto, ON M5W 1G2, CANADA • (416) 777-2755 • Web site: www.clga.ca/archives

Collects and maintains information and materials relating to the gay and lesbian rights movement in Canada and elsewhere. Its collection of records and other materials documenting the stories of lesbians and gay men and their organizations in Canada is available to the public for the purpose of education and research. It also publishes an annual newsletter, *Lesbian and Gay Archivist.*

Children of Gays and Lesbians Everywhere (COLAGE)

3543 18th St., Suite 1, San Francisco, CA 94110 • (415) 861-5437 • Fax: (415) 255-8345 • e-mail: collage@ colage.org • Web site: www.colage.org

COLAGE is a national and international organization that supports young people with lesbian, gay, bisexual, and transgender (LGBT) parents. Their mission is to foster the growth of daughters and sons of LGBT parents by providing education, support, and community. Their publications include such newsletters as *Tips for Making Classrooms Safer for Students With LGBT Parents* and *COLAGE Summary*.

Concerned Women for America (CWFA)

1015 15th St. NW, Suite 1100, Washington, DC 20005 • (202) 488-7000 • Fax: (202) 488-0806 • e-mail: mail@ cwfa.org • Web site: www.cwfa.org

The CWFA is an educational and legal defense foundation that seeks to strengthen the traditional family by promoting Judeo-Christian moral standards. It opposes gay marriage and the granting of additional civil rights protections to gays and lesbians. The CWFA publishes the monthly magazine *Family Voice* and various position papers on gay marriage and other issues.

Courage

c/o Church of St. John the Baptist, 210 W. 31st St., New York, NY 10001 • (212) 268-1010 • Fax: (212) 268-7150 • e-mail: NYCourage@aol.com • Web site: http:// CourageRC.net

Courage is a network of spiritual support groups for gay and lesbian Catholics who wish to lead celibate lives in accordance with Roman Catholic teachings on homosexuality. It publishes listings of local groups, a newsletter, and an annotated bibliography of books on homosexuality.

Equal Rights Marriage Fund (ERMF)

2001 M St. NW, Washington, DC 20036 • (202) 822-6546 • Fax: (202) 466-3540

The ERMF is dedicated to the legalization of gay and lesbian marriage and serves as a national clearinghouse for information on same-sex marriage. The organization publishes several brochures and articles, including *Gay Marriage: A Civil Right*.

Family Research Council (FRC)

700 13th St. NW, Suite 500, Washington, DC 20005 • (202) 393-2100 • Fax: (202) 393-2134

The council is a research, resource, and educational organization that promotes the traditional family, which the council defines as a group of people bound by marriage, blood, or adoption. The council opposes gay marriage and adoption rights. It publishes numerous reports from a conservative perspective on issues affecting the family, including homosexuality. These publications include the monthly newsletter *Washington Watch* and bimonthly journal *Family Policy*.

Family Research Institute (FRI)

PO Box 62640, Colorado Springs, CO 80962-0640 • (303) 681-3113 • Web site: www.familyresearchinst.org

The FRI distributes information about family, sexuality, and substance abuse issues. It believes that strengthening marriage would reduce many social problems, including crime, poverty, and sexually transmitted diseases. The institute publishes the bimonthly newsletter *Family Research Report* as well as the position paper "What's Wrong with Gay Marriage?"

Focus on the Family

8605 Explorer Dr., Colorado Springs, CO 80920 • (800) 232-6459 • Fax: (719) 548-4525 • Web site: www.family.org

Focus on the Family is a conservative Christian organization that promotes traditional family values and gender roles. Its publications include the monthly magazine *Focus on the Family* and the reports "Setting the Record Straight: What Research Really Says About the Social Consequences of Homosexuality," "No-Fault Fallout: The Grim Aftermath of Modern Divorce Law and How to Change It," "Only a Piece of Paper? The Unquestionable Benefits of Lifelong Marriage," and "'Only a Piece of Paper?' The Social Significance of the Marriage License and the Negative Consequences of Cohabitation."

Howard Center for Family, Religion, and Society
934 North Main St., Rockford, IL 61103 • (815) 964-5819 • Fax: (815) 965-1826 • Web site: http://profam.org/Default.htm

The purpose of the Howard Center is to provide research and understanding that demonstrates and affirms family and religion as the foundation of a virtuous and free society. The Center believes that the natural family is the fundamental unit of society. The primary mission of the Howard Center is to provide a clearinghouse of useful and relevant information to support families and their defenders throughout the world. The Center publishes the monthly journal, *Family in America,* and the *Religion and Society Report.*

Human Rights Campaign (HRC)
919 18th St., NW, Suite 800, Washington, DC 20006 • (202) 628-4160 • Fax: (202) 347-5323 • Web site: www.hrc.org

The HRC provides information on national political issues affecting lesbian, gay, bisexual, and transgender Americans. It offers resources to educate congressional leaders and the public on critical issues such as ending workplace discrimination, combating hate crimes, fighting HIV/AIDS, protecting gay and lesbian families, and working for better lesbian health. HRC publishes the HRC *Quarterly* and *LAWbriefs*.

IntiNet Resource Center
PO Box 4322, San Rafael, CA 94913 • e-mail: pad@well.com

The center promotes non-monogamous relationships as an alternative to the traditional family. It also serves as a clearinghouse for information on non-monogamous relationships and as a network for people interested in alternative family lifestyles. IntiNet publishes the quarterly newsletter *Floodtide*, the book *Polyamory: The New Love Without Limits*, and the *Resource Guide for the Responsible Non-Monogamist*.

Lambda Legal Defense and Education Fund, Inc.
666 Broadway, Suite 1200, New York, NY 10012 • (212) 995-8585 • Fax: (212) 995-2306

Lambda is a public-interest law firm committed to achieving full recognition of the civil rights of lesbians, gay men, and people with HIV/AIDS. The firm addresses a variety of areas, including equal marriage rights, the military, parenting and relationship issues, and domestic-partner benefits. It publishes the quarterly *Lambda Update* and the pamphlet *Freedom to Marry*.

Loving More
PO Box 4358, Boulder, CO 80306 • (303) 534-7540 • e-mail: ryan@lovemore.com. • Web site: www.lovemore.com

Loving More explores and supports many different forms of family and relationships. It promotes alternative relationship options—such as open marriage, extended family, and multi-partner marriages—and serves as a national clearinghouse for the multi-partner movement. The organization publishes the quarterly magazine *Loving More*.

National Center for Lesbian Rights

870 Market St., Suite 570, San Francisco, CA 94102 •
(415) 392-6257 • Fax: (415) 392-8442

The center is a public-interest law office providing legal counseling and representation for victims of sexual-orientation discrimination. Primary areas of advice include child custody and parenting, employment, housing, the military, and insurance. Among the center's publications are the handbooks *Recognizing Lesbian and Gay Families: Strategies for Obtaining Domestic Partners Benefits and Lesbian and Gay Parenting: A Psychological and Legal Perspective*.

National Gay and Lesbian Task Force (NGLTF)

2320 17th St. NW, Washington, DC 20009-2702 • (202) 332-6483 • Fax: (202) 332-0207

NGLTF is a civil-rights advocacy organization that lobbies Congress and the White House on a range of civil rights and AIDS issues. The organization is working to make same-sex marriage legal. It publishes numerous papers and pamphlets, and the booklet *To Have and to Hold: Organizing for Our Right to Marry* and the fact sheet "Lesbian and Gay Families."

The Rockford Institute Center on the Family in America

934 N. Main St., Rockford, IL 61103 • (815) 964-5811•
Fax: (815) 965-1826

The Rockford Institute works to return America to Judeo-Christian values and supports traditional roles for men and women. Its Center on the Family in America studies the evolution of the family and the effects of divorce on society. The institute publishes *Family in America* and *Chronicles*, both of which are monthly periodicals, and the newsletter *Main Street Memorandum*.

Traditional Values Coalition
139 C St. SE, Washington, DC 20003 • (202) 547-8570
• Fax: (202) 546-6403

The coalition strives to restore what the group believes are traditional moral and spiritual values in American government, schools, media, and the fiber of American society. It believes that gay rights threaten the family unit and extend civil rights beyond what the coalition considers appropriate limits. The coalition publishes the quarterly newsletter *Traditional Values Report,* as well as various information papers, one of which specifically addresses same-sex marriage.

Bibliography

Books

Sean Cahill, *Same Sex Marriage in the United States: Focus on the Facts*. Lanham: Lexington Books, 2004.

George Chauncey, *Why Marriage?: The History Shaping Today's Debate Over Gay Equality*. Cambridge, MA: Basic Books, 2004.

James Dobson, *Marriage Under Fire: Why We Must Win This Battle*. Sisters, OR: Multnomah Publishers, Inc., 2004.

Ronnie W. Floyd, *The Gay Agenda: It's Dividing the Family, the Church, and a Nation*. Green Forest, AR: New Leaf Press, 2004.

Lauri S. Friedman, ed., *Introducing Issues with Opposing Viewpoints: Gay Marriage*. San Diego: Greenhaven Press, 2006.

Abigail Garner, *Families Like Mine: Children of Gay Parents Tell It Like It Is*. New York: HarperCollins, 2004.

Evan Gerstmann, *Same-Sex Marriage and the Constitution*. New York: Cambridge University Press, 2004.

E.J. Graff, *What is Marriage For?: The Strange Social History of Our Most Intimate Institution*. Boston: Beacon Press, 1999.

Noelle Howey et al., *Out of the Ordinary: Essays on Growing Up With Gay, Lesbian, and Transgender Parents*. New York: Stonewall Inn Editions, 2000.

Davina Kotulski, *Why You Should Give A Damn About Gay Marriage*. Los Angeles: Advocate Books, 2004.

Erwin W. Lutzer, *The Truth About Same-Sex Marriage: 6 Things You Need to Know About What's Really at Stake*. Chicago: Moody Publishers, 2004. A Christian argument against gay marriage.

David Moats, *Civil Wars: A Battle for Gay Marriage.* Orlando: Harcourt, 2004. Written by a Pulitzer-Prize winning journalist, this book chronicles the struggle over marriage since 2000.

Jonathan Rauch, *Gay Marriage: Why It Is Good for Gays, Good for Straights, and Good for America.* New York: Times Books-Henry Holt & Company, 2004.

Alan Sears and Craig Osten, *The Homosexual Agenda: Exposing the Principal Threat to Religious Freedom Today.* Nashville, TN: Broadman & Holman Publishers, 2003.

Peter Sprigg, *Outrage: How Gay Activists and Liberal Judges Are Trashing Democracy to Redefine Marriage.* Washington D.C.: Regnery Publishing, 2004.

Glenn T. Stanton and Bill Maier, *Marriage on Trial: The Case Against Same-Sex Marriage and Parenting.* Downers Grove, IL: InterVarsity Press, 2004.

Andrew Sullivan, *Same-Sex Marriage: Pro and Con: A Reader.* New York:

Greg Wharton and Ian Philips, *I do/I Don't: Queers on Marriage.* San Francisco: Suspect Thoughts Press: 2004.

Evan Wolfson, *Why Marriage Matters: America, Equality, and Gay People's Right to Marry.* New York: Simon & Schuster, 2004.

Periodicals

"Render unto Caesar; Liberty v. equality," *Economist,* January 27, 2007, p. 12.

Against the Current, "Gay Marriage, Yes!" May/June 2004.

David Aikman, "Train wreck coming: why homosexual marriage threatens free expression of religion," *Christianity Today,* Oct 2006.

Kurt Andersen, "The gay-wedding present; Don't call off the caterer just yet: New York's same-sex-marriage court defeat is a gift in disguise," *New York*, July 24, 2006, p 14.

Ryan T. Anderson, "Beyond Gay Marriage; The stated goal of these prominent gay activists is no longer merely the freedom to live as they want," *Weekly Standard*, August 15, 2006.

Robert Benne and Gerald McDermott, "Gay Unions Undermine Society," *The Roanoke Times*, February 22, 2004.

Christopher S. Bentley, "The Assault on Marriage," *The New American*, April 19, 2004.

Mark David Blum, "A Matter of Personal Freedom: What's Love Got to Do With State-Sanctioned Marriage?" *The Post-Standard (Syracuse, NY)*, December 2, 2004.

Victoria A. Brownworth, "Civil Disobedience—Civil Rights," *Curve*, Vol. 14, June 2004.

Patrick J. Buchanan, "Time for a New Boston Tea Party," *The Wanderer*, December 4, 2003.

William F. Buckley Jr, "Gay impasse," *National Review*, December 4, 2006, p. 58.

Nadine Chaffee, "One Son's Choice: Love or Country? Our reluctance to accept gay marriage forces people to move away from their homes and their families," *Newsweek*, February 5, 2007, p 22.

Charles Colson, "Societal Suicide: Legalizing Gay Marriage Will Lead to More Family Breakdown and Crime," *Christianity Today*, June 2004.

Bryan Cones, "Extending family: is there really only one way to make a Catholic household?" *U.S. Catholic*, September 2006, p 50.

Judith Davidoff, "No wedding bells: why banning same-sex marriage spells disaster," *Progressive*, August 2006, p 22.

George Detweiler, "How to Protect Marriage," *The New American*, August 9, 2004.

James C. Dobson, "Two Mommies Is One Too Many," *Time*, December 18, 2006, p 123.

James Driscoll, "New Gay Political Strategies: Better Results Call for Better Leadership," *The Washington Times*, November 18, 2004.

Kevin Duchschere, "Is Gay Marriage a Civil-Rights Issue? Five Black Leaders Say It's Not Same," *Star Tribune (Minneapolis, MN)*, March 26, 2004.

Lisa Duggan, "Holy Matrimony," *Nation*, March 15, 2004.

The Economist, "The Case for Gay Marriage," February 28, 2004.

Richard A. Epstein, "Live and Let Live," *Wall Street Journal*, July 13, 2004.

Nathaniel Frank, "Perverted—Quack Gay Marriage Science," *The New Republic*, May 3, 2004.

Robert P. George and David L. Tubbs, "Redefining Marriage Away," *City Journal*, Summer 2004.

Paul Greenberg, "Gay Marriage and its Discontents," *Conservative Chronicle*, April 7, 2004.

Kim Grossnicklaus, "Gay Marriages Deprive the Children," *The Register-Guard (Eugene, OR)*, March 8, 2004.

Sadie Fields, "The Gay Marriage Amendment: Can't Let the Few Hurt Society as a Whole," *The Atlanta Journal-Constitution*, October 25, 2004.

Thomas M. Keane, Jr., "Not Every Church Fears Gay Marriage," *The Boston Herald*, February 11, 2004.

Douglas R. Kmiec, "Family Matters," *Los Angeles Times*, March 14, 2004.

Hank Kalet, "Tying the Knot: First Step in Massachusetts," *Progressive Populist*, June 15, 2004.

David Limbaugh, "'Gay Marriage' Is Not About 'Rights,'" *Townhall.com*, February 27, 2004.

Los Angeles Times, "The Meaning of Marriage," July 16, 2004.

Howard Manly, "Gay vs. Civil Rights Fight Misses Point," *The Boston Herald*, March 9, 2004.

Karla Mantilla, "Gay Marriage: Destroying the Family to Save the Children?" *Off Our Backs*, May-June 2004.

Edwin Meese, "A Shotgun Amendment," *Wall Street Journal*, March 10, 2004.

Scott Michels, "For Gays, New Math," *U.S. News & World Report*, August 14, 2006, p34-36.

Irene Monroe, "A tale of two Marys," *The Advocate*, January 30, 2007, p 64.

Mark Morford, "Where is My Gay Apocalypse?" *SFGate.com*, March 5, 2004.

Tiffany L. Palmer, "Family Matters: Establishing Legal Parental Rights for Same-Sex Parents and Their Children," *Human Rights*, Summer 2003.

Robert W. Patterson, "Why Gay Marriage Doesn't Measure Up," *Human Events*, March 22, 2004.

Ramesh Ponnuru, "Coming Out Ahead: Why Gay Marriage is on the Way," *National Review*, July 28, 2003.

Deb Price, "Sullying the Constitution An Affront to All," *Liberal Opinion Week*, March 15, 2004.

Jonathan Rauch, "Power of Two," *The New York Times Magazine*, March 7, 2004.

The Register-Guard (Eugene, OR), "Leave Constitution Alone," February 25, 2004.

Revolutionary Worker, "The Insane Ravings of the Marriage Police," August 17, 2003.

Jim Rinnert, "The Trouble with Gay Marriage," *In These Times*, January 19, 2004.

Rocky Mountain News (Denver, CO), "Who Decides Gay Marriage?" March 7, 2004.

William Rusher, "Let the States Decide What 'Marriage' Is," *WorldNetDaily.com*, March 4, 2004.

Amelia Saletan, "Less Sanctimony, More Matrimony," *Benladner.com*, January 25, 2004.

Rick Santorum, "Defend Marriage Now," *Crisis Magazine*, September 1, 2003.

Brad Sears and Alan Hirsch, "Straight-Out Truth on Gay Parents," *Los Angeles Times*, April 4, 2004.

Sharon Slater, "How Does Legalizing Same-Sex Marriage Hurt Marriage, Children and Society?" *Meridian Magazine*, 2004.

Shelby Steele, "Selma to San Francisco?" *Wall Street Journal*, March 18, 2004.

Mark Steyn, "Marital Strife," *National Review*, December 22, 2003.

Lynne Stoecklein, "Love is Blind," *The Denver Post*, April 11, 2004.

Trevor Thomas, "Someday, I Want to Get Married: Gay Marriage Should Be Debated in Human Terms," *The Grand Rapids Press*, July 25, 2004.

Thomas Tryon, "Conservative Arguments Compel Support for Gay Marriage," *Sarasota Herald Tribune*, March 14, 2004.

Norah Vincent, "Gays Won't Tear Marriage Asunder," *Los Angeles Times*, July 17, 2003.

David M. Wagner, "Gay Marriage Lite; New Jersey's high court doesn't quite go all the way." *Weekly Standard*, November 6, 2006.

WebSites

Alliance For Marriage (www.allianceformarriage.org/site/PageServer). A non-profit organization devoted to traditional family values and opposes gay marriage. The website includes news updates, articles, speeches and information on the proposed Federal Marriage Amendment, which was written and heavily lobbied for by Alliance For Marriage.

American Family Association (www.afa.net). Dedicated to preserving traditional family values and rejecting gay marriage, abortion, pornography, and gambling. A section on Special Projects details their ongoing boycotts of companies they believe threaten family values.

Don'tAmend.com (www.dontamend.com). DontAmend.com is a web campaign that was launched in 2003 to prevent the Constitution from being amended to specify marriage as an institution between a man and a woman. Contains up-to-date information on protest events and rallies to halt the proposed amendment and gay-marriage-related news around the country.

Equal Marriage for Same-Sex Couples (www.samesex-marriage.ca). This exhaustive pro-gay marriage website is based in Canada, where same-sex marriage became legal in 2005. Includes news updates, articles, history, legal briefs, and more.

Human Rights Campaign (www.hrc.org). Human Rights Campaign is America's largest gay and lesbian organization, and works to secure rights for gays, lesbians, bisexuals, and transgendered individuals. The website includes a section on issues surrounding gay marriage.

Index

Picture Credits

About the Editor

Lauri S. Friedman earned her bachelor's degree in religion and political science from Vassar College in Poughkeepsie, NY. Her studies there focused on political Islam. Friedman has worked as a non-fiction writer, a newspaper journalist, and an editor for more than 7 years. She has accumulated extensive experience in both academic and professional settings.

Friedman has edited and authored numerous publications for Greenhaven Press on controversial social issues such as gay marriage, Islam, energy, discrimination, suicide bombers, and the war on terror. Much of the Writing the Critical Essay series has been under her direction or authorship. She was instrumental in the creation of the series, and played a critical role in its conception and development.